SAVIOR

ALSO BY MAGREY R. DEVEGA:

Almost Christmas

Awaiting the Already

Embracing the Uncertain

One Faithful Promise

Hope for Hard Times

SAVIOR

What the Bible Says

about the Cross

MAGREY R. deVEGA

Abingdon Press / Nashville

SAVIOR
What the Bible Says about the Cross

Copyright © 2020 Abingdon Press
All rights reserved.

Library of Congress Control Number: 2020945165
ISBN 978-1-5018-8099-5

20 21 22 23 24 25 26 27 28 29—10 9 8 7 6 5 4 3 2 1
MANUFACTURED IN THE UNITED STATES OF AMERICA

To Bruce, Paul, and Rita,
for teaching me the way of
faithfulness, humility, and love;

To the people of
Hyde Park United Methodist Church,
for modeling how to love God and love all;

And to my family,
especially Maddy and Grace.

CONTENTS

CONTENTS

INTRODUCTION

One of the annual highlights of my being a pastor is "Ask the Pastor" night, when I field questions from our fourth- and fifth-graders. I always find their questions to be both playful and curious, including questions like these: Can you recite the alphabet backward in under thirty seconds? Have you ever solved a Rubik's Cube? What made you want to be a pastor? How do you come up with your sermons?

Along with this playfulness, many of their questions cut right to the heart of some of the more challenging difficulties of the Christian faith. Inevitably I am asked these kinds of questions: Why do innocent people suffer? Where do we go when we die? How can we explain the Trinity? How do we pray, and how do we know it's doing any good?

One time, a student asked a question that pretty much summarized it all: How do I know if I truly believe?

I remember answering the question the best I could, talking about the relationship between belief and behavior. Belief ought to shape our behavior, I said, just as James said that "faith without works is dead." And I said it works the other way too. Sometimes, when we struggle to believe, we need to *practice* that belief until we are able to believe it.

The students were receptive to that answer, for the most part. But then it opened a whole series of other questions: Is it okay to doubt? Have you ever struggled with your faith? What if I'm not sure what to believe?

I love the courage it takes to ask those kinds of questions, regardless of the age of the person asking them. I've even asked them myself, many times over the years.

It's in these times that I like to remember that our relationship with God is in some ways like a relationship with anyone else: it changes over time.

Think about your relationship with your parents. When you were much younger, you may have depended on them for provision, guidance, and discipline. As you grew older, you might have asserted your independence, even quarreled with them, and sought some distance from them. And now, perhaps in your older years, you have come to appreciate them in a different way and maybe drawn closer to them than before. Relationships change.

If you've been married for a while, you know that your relationship with your spouse is quite different from when you first met. Early in your courtship, everything felt new and exciting, as you explored every interesting nuance and possibility in your budding romance. But as time has gone by, through events that range from the mundane to the heartbreaking, your perception of the other person, and the maturity of your relationship, is fuller, more complicated, and richer.

Our relationship with God is the same in this regard as the relationships we have with the most important people in our lives. Not only is it allowed to change, it is expected to.

It's not necessarily because God changes, but because we do. Our situations change. We learn and gain experience. We develop new habits and relationships. And each time those things happen, our understanding of God enters a critical phase. We aren't sure if what we once believed still holds, or whether we will have to walk away from belief altogether.

At the very least, the stretching of our belief is painful and uncertain, and we can't see any possible benefits. But there are benefits. It's a lot like a growth spurt in our bones or the tearing of muscle fibers so they grow back stronger. Sometimes the Spirit uses our experiences to push us into broader, richer, and deeper understandings of God.

This book focuses on one of the most common areas of the Christian faith in which we experience such growth spurts, the one that is most central to our beliefs: the work of Jesus on the cross. These growth spurts surface in such questions as: Why did Jesus have to die? How exactly does Jesus save us? And what does that mean for our belief and our behavior?

Those fourth- and fifth-graders have asked it this way:

- Why did Jesus have to die to forgive our sins? Couldn't God just forgive us?
- How exactly did the blood of Jesus save us?
- Did God plan the death of Jesus?

Children and youth are not the only ones that ask these questions. Many adults do as well, perhaps more than once as their belief stretches and their relationship with God changes.

I think about a person who has been a Christian for many years, but now wonders if the image of blood sacrifice is at all relevant today.

I think of a person who is troubled by the violence of the cross, seeing it as a reinforcement of our cultural addiction to bloodshed that is all around us.

I think about a person whose childhood relationship with a father was one of heartache and abuse, who has trouble believing that God would sacrifice Jesus. That person would see such an act as heartless and cruel.

I think of a person caught in an abusive relationship, who struggles with Jesus's call to "take up your cross." If Jesus willingly submitted himself to suffering and punishment, does that mean we are to do the same?

I think of a person who is so beset by shame and guilt, a broken spirit, or addictive, self-destructive behavior that it is impossible to see how Jesus can help overcome them.

WHAT DOES THE CROSS MEAN?

In a way, these people are wrestling with some pretty foundational questions, and you may be too. The cross, after all, is the central symbol of the Christian faith. But what does it mean? What exactly did Jesus do to save us from our sins? Why was the cross necessary, and what does it mean to us today? What is it about the way Jesus died that offers salvation for us? Why did Jesus do what he did, and what does that mean for us? And how can answers to these questions help us as our faith stretches and grows?

Throughout its history, the church has developed numerous answers to those questions, under the broad theological term *atonement*. No single image or framework can possibly capture a mystery as great as Jesus's death on the cross. The Bible uses many different metaphors to describe what happened on the cross and how it brings us salvation, and several theories over the centuries have brought these metaphors together in different ways to shed light on Jesus's death and its meaning. Studying each of these theories ought to be more than just an intellectual thought exercise. It can deepen our love for God and others and strengthen our commitment to follow Jesus.

This book will not only be useful for anyone who wishes to understand the meaning of Jesus's death but also will be particularly helpful for anyone whose life situation is prompting a "crisis of faith" in relation to Jesus and the cross.

Throughout these pages, we will explore together various biblical metaphors for how Jesus's death brings atonement, as well as the larger frameworks theologians have used to bring them together. Along the way, it is my hope that you will encounter something new enough to you to offer novel, life-giving possibilities to your faith journey. If you're going through such a "crisis of faith," these new ways of seeing the cross may allow you to have a fuller, richer, and deeper view of God's love for you, much like viewing a color television for the first time when you have only seen black and white, or seeing in three dimensions when all you have known is two. And if you are not experiencing such a crisis, exploring various understandings of Jesus's death, all rooted in Scripture, will offer you a clearer picture of the hope you have in Christ.

Each week, as you explore different approaches to the atonement, you'll develop a greater awareness of your own sin and an appreciation for God's faithful love. And, you'll discern ways to translate your beliefs about the cross into concrete ways to follow Jesus.

As the journey unfolds in the pages ahead, may you be enriched by the rich tapestry of perspectives and images regarding Christ's work on the cross. May your understanding of the cross be deepened, your behavior shaped by the Holy Spirit, and your commitment to Christ be strengthened.

Ultimately, may you be inspired by God's love for you, revealed in Jesus Christ.

CHAPTER 1

SUBSTITUTION: JESUS TAKES YOUR PLACE

CHAPTER 1

SUBSTITUTION:
JESUS TAKES YOUR PLACE

1 Peter 2:20-24 • Romans 3:23-26

A trembling soul, I sought the Lord,
My sin confessed, my guilt deplored;
How soft and sweet, his word to me,
"I took thy place, and died for thee."
Eliza E. Hewitt, "He Took My Place"

In the Rijksmuseum in Amsterdam is a print in etching and drypoint called *The Three Crosses* by the famous Dutch artist Rembrandt van Rijn. It is a powerful depiction of Jesus on the cross, with the two thieves on each side. It is composed with stark grays and blacks, except for the beam of light shining from the heavens, signifying the inbreaking of God's holiness cast into a world of sin.

But what's most fascinating about this painting can be found off on the side. In the dark shadows of the crosses, off in the fringe of the painting, is a figure. He is barely recognizable, face buried in his hands, overcome with emotion.

3

The identity of this figure is debated, but some have concluded that this humble, grieving person is none other than Rembrandt himself, whom he painted into this scene in stirring recognition of his own role in Jesus's crucifixion. He acknowledged that he was responsible for the very sins that ultimately put Jesus on the cross. In that self-portrait Rembrandt was expressing not just feelings of grief and guilt, but ultimately also of gratitude. For Jesus had taken his place and done something that he could not do for himself.

That is at the heart of the idea of substitutionary atonement, the most prevalent understanding of the cross among most Christians today.

Substitutionary atonement is the idea that Jesus saved us by taking our place, bearing the fate that we deserved. It is an appropriate starting point for our journey together.

A WORLD BASED ON RULES

The framework of substitutionary atonement is built on the idea that actions have consequences, and wrongful actions deserve punishment. This is a concept, after all, that we learn at any early age, from our parents and our teachers: live by the rules, and you'll be okay. Break them, and you will cause harm to yourself and others. Think about the times you've learned lessons like these. If you don't look both ways before crossing the street, you might get hurt. If you touch a hot stove, you will get burned. If you don't wear a coat outside when it's cold, you might get sick.

If you act within the guidelines, you'll usually be fine. If you don't, things will go wrong. This principle is not just a handy precept to teach our kids. It is based on a fundamental view of the world and an understanding of the way life ought to work. And this idea influences our concepts of justice and fairness. It is the idea that if there is to be order and decency in the world, then the guilty must be punished in order for wrongs to be righted. Those are the rules; changing them will cause nothing but chaos and anarchy.

In the popular comic strip *Calvin and Hobbes*, by Bill Watterson, young Calvin and his best friend Hobbes often play their favorite game, "Calvinball."[1] It is a game whose only permanent rule, according to Calvin, is "that you can't play it the same way twice." Each time they play, Calvin and Hobbes up the ante on spontaneous, often ludicrous rules in the middle of the game, like opposite poles, time-fracture wickets, the "very sorry song," and the "invisible sector." Final scores are just as meaningless as the rules themselves, with games ending with "oogy to boogy" and "Q to 12."

Watterson said, "People have asked me how to play Calvinball. It's pretty simple: you make up the rules as you go."

Now, it's one thing for a six-year old boy with a clever imagination to play a game with inconsistent rules. But it's hard to imagine a world where Calvinball is the order of the day, in which the rules change on a whim, and the only steady, reliable idea is that no rules are permanent.

So, much of the first five books of the Bible, which we know as the Torah, are the Israelites' counter to a Calvinball worldview. In particular, the books of Exodus, Leviticus, Numbers, and Deuteronomy spell out in vivid detail the rules for right and proper living in relation to God and to other people.

There are 613 commandments, to be exact, with Jewish tradition claiming that the 365 "negative" commandments ("Thou shalt not…") correspond to the same number of days of the solar year, and the remaining 248 "positive commandments ("Thou shalt...") correspond to the number of bones in the human body.[2] In total, it is the instruction manual for how one is to live. Keep these commandments, and you will live. But break these commandments, and there must be a punishment.

In Calvinball, the worst that happens is that Calvin and Hobbes feud and bicker over who won. But in life, breaking the rules requires restitution, or the whole order of the world falls apart.

But to take it one step even further, when humans break the rules that God has established, it is not just human beings that are on the line. It is God's very character and commitment to justice that is on trial. For if we believe the first thing we learn about God in Genesis, which is that God's primary activity in the world is to bring order out of chaos and that God's intent for this broken world is that it be restored back to its original state of goodness, perfection, and holiness, then it is God's resolve that is called into question whenever human beings sin.

So, that is where Jesus enters the picture.

> *What Jesus performed was a self-sacrifice,*
> *a willingness to assume for us the*
> *punishment that we deserved so*
> *that we would not have to.*

"No one has greater love," Jesus said in John's Gospel, "than to give up one's life for one's friends" (15:13). What happened on the cross was not just a sacrifice, used to fulfill an ancient blood atonement system. What Jesus performed was a self-sacrifice, a willingness to assume for us the punishment that we deserved so that we would not have to. Or to express it another way, a willingness to pay an infinite price, which no human is capable of paying, to satisfy the debt we owe to God for our sin.

SUBSTITUTING YOUR NAME

One of the more vivid stories involving substitutionary atonement is from the evangelical publishing company Bible Truth Ministries, which tells the story of John Coutts, a nineteenth-century sea captain. An irreligious person throughout his life, Captain Coutts contracted an illness while on board his vessel. He was not ready to die.

Desperate, Coutts sent for his first mate, a man named Williams, and ordered him to pray for him. But Williams refused, admitting to his captain that he did not know how to pray. Coutts then ordered Williams to retrieve for him a Bible, which Williams refused a second time, acknowledging that he was not a religious man.

Coutts then called for the second mate, a man named Palmer, hoping that he could be of help. "Palmer, I'm not going to get better," Coutts told him, "and I'm not going to last until we reach port. I want you to pray for me. Ask God to have mercy on my sinful soul." But the second mate responded in the same way, saying he did not know how to pray and that he also did not own a Bible.

The captain then ordered that the whole vessel be searched for one person who could pray for the captain or provide him with a Bible. Finally, one of the sailors identified a young helper in the galley named Willie Platt.

The sailor asked him, "Willie, do you have a Bible?"

"Yes, sir," Willie responded. "But I only read it on my own time."

"Don't worry. Just get the Bible and go to the captain's cabin. He's dying and wants a Bible."

Willie reported to the captain, Bible in hand. The captain acknowledged that his time was limited, and that he was sorry for the sins of his past. He asked Willie to pray that God would have mercy on him and that he might read something from the Bible that might offer him comfort.

Willie remembered a passage from Isaiah 53 that his mother had read to him before he left home. He read to the captain verses 4-6, about how Jesus bore the captain's sins so that he did not have to bear them himself:

> *It was certainly our sickness that he carried,*
> *and our sufferings that he bore,*
> *but we thought him afflicted,*
> *struck down by God and tormented.*
> *He was pierced because of our rebellions*
> *and crushed because of our crimes.*
> *He bore the punishment that made us whole;*
> *by his wounds we are healed.*
> *Like sheep we had all wandered away,*
> *each going its own way,*
> *but the LORD let fall on him all our crimes.*

The captain, realizing the power of those words, and the promise of his salvation that they contained, ordered Willie to read the words again. "Stop, boy!" he cried. "That sounds like it! Read it again."

Willie read the passage a second time. And the captain responded, "Aye, that's good—that's it, I'm sure."

Sensing the wave of openness and relief that was settling into the captain's heart. Willie Platt went further. "Captain, when I was reading that verse at home, my mother made me put my name in it. May I read it to you that way?"

"Yes, boy," the captain said. Put your name in right where your mother told you, and read it to me again."

"It was certainly [Willie's] sickness that he carried," Willie recited, reading the whole passage, and concluding with, "by his wounds [Willie] is healed."

The captain, with a growing peace in his heart, asked Willie to read it once more, but this time substituting the captain's own name in the passage.

"It was certainly [John's] sickness that he carried...by his wounds [John] is healed."

The captain dismissed Willie, closed his eyes, repeating the words of Isaiah 53:5 in his mind and heart, substituting his own name into the passage, even as he acknowledged that Jesus Christ had substituted himself for the captain. With that sense of peace washing over him, the Captain John Coutts eventually passed away, recognizing his Savior, grateful for what he had done for him.[3]

SUBSTITUTIONARY ATONEMENT IN THE BIBLE AND HISTORY

The power of that story explains why substitutionary atonement has been so popular and prevalent throughout the history of the church. Many Christian thinkers have understood the cross in this way, with Anselm of Canterbury (1033–1109) being one of the most influential. Anselm drew on the legal ideas of his own days, especially those surrounding debt and how to repay or satisfy debt, to explain why substitutionary atonement was necessary. Ultimately, he said, it was the character of God that was at stake, and this amounted to an infinite debt that must be repaid:

> But God cannot properly leave anything uncorrected in His kingdom. Furthermore, to leave sin unpunished would be tantamount to treating the sinful and the sinless alike, which would be inconsistent with God's nature. And this inconsistency is injustice. It is necessary, therefore, that either the honour taken away should be repaid, or punishment should be inflicted.[4]

Later, the reformer John Calvin (1509–1564) grounded his understanding of the atonement on Anselm's work, describing how Jesus Christ was the only suitable substitute for the punishment that was meant for human beings:

> Therefore, our Lord came forth very man, adopted the person of Adam, and assumed his name, that he might in his stead obey the Father; that he might present our flesh as the price of satisfaction to the just judgment of God, and in the same flesh pay the penalty which we had incurred.[5]

Advocates of substitutionary atonement draw their support from the deep well of biblical texts, particularly in the Old Testament. There we see the central role that the sacrificial system, and blood atonement in particular, played in the righting of human injustice. In the Torah, we see how the worldview of the Israelites was governed by the idea that when we are separated from God, then something has to die in order to bring us back into a relationship with God. One way to interpret God's acceptance of Abel's offering, and not that of his brother Cain, is to recognize that Abel's offering was an animal and therefore it involved the shedding of blood. Though we may find God's favor of Abel odd because the sacrificial laws had not yet been introduced, it was an early indication that for humans to be in right and proper relationship to God, something had to die.

Skip ahead to Exodus, and we remember the story of how the Israelites were held captive in Egypt under the oppression of Pharaoh. And what was the final act of God that finally guaranteed freedom for the Israelite slaves? The killing of the firstborn males in Egypt, with the exception of those Israelites who sprinkled a lamb's blood on their doorposts. And when the angel of death passed over those houses where an animal's blood had been spilled, those people were saved from punishment. The blood of the lamb assured that the people in that household would be spared.

And then, of course, there is much of the rest of the Pentateuch—Leviticus, Numbers, and Deuteronomy—in which God gave the Israelites detailed instructions on how to make blood sacrifices in order to satisfy the punishment that was due to humans because of their sin. In particular, there are texts like Numbers 15, which cover even the sins that are committed unintentionally:

> *If an individual sins unintentionally, that person must present a one-year-old female goat for a purification offering. The priest will seek reconciliation in the LORD's presence for the person who sinned unintentionally, when the sin is an accident, seeking reconciliation so that person will be forgiven. There will be one set of instructions for the Israelite citizen and the immigrant residing with you for anyone who commits an unintentional sin. (vv. 27-29)*

11

By the time we get to the New Testament, and the authors of the Gospels and Epistles began to reflect on what the cross means for the world, most of them did so through the lens of that ancient sacrificial practice. They interpreted passages like Isaiah 53 in much the same way as Captain John Coutts did, understanding Jesus as the one who suffered on our behalf, and his blood became the suitable satisfaction of the punishment that we deserved or a repayment of the debt we owed. Consider these passages from the Epistles:

> *He carried in his own body on the cross the sins we committed. He did this so that we might live in righteousness, having nothing to do with sin. By his wounds you were healed.*
>
> *(1 Peter 2:24)*

> *Christ redeemed us from the curse of the Law by becoming a curse for us—because it is written,* Everyone who is hung on a tree is cursed. *He redeemed us so that the blessing of Abraham would come to the Gentiles through Christ Jesus, and that we would receive the promise of the Spirit through faith.*
>
> *(Galatians 3:13-14)*

> *God caused the one who didn't know sin to be sin for our sake so that through him we could become the righteousness of God.*
>
> *(2 Corinthians 5:21)*

SUBSTITUTIONARY ATONEMENT IN SONG

Many of our great hymn writers understood the work of the cross in this way, vividly portraying the Crucifixion to underscore the shedding of Christ's blood as a way of eliciting gratitude that Jesus took our place. The most stirring example is "O Sacred Head, Now Wounded":

> O sacred Head, now wounded,
> with grief and shame weighed down
> now scornfully surrounded
> with thorns, thine only crown....
>
> What thou, my Lord, hast suffered
> was all for sinners' gain;
> mine, mine was the transgression,
> but thine the deadly pain.[6]

Even brighter and more triumphant hymns like "To God Be the Glory" give a nod to the substitutionary work of Jesus, using legal and courtroom language to explain how Jesus assumed the punishment that was ours to bear:

> O perfect redemption, the purchase of blood,
> to every believer the promise of God;
> the vilest offender who truly believes,
> that moment from Jesus a pardon receives.
>
> Praise the Lord, praise the Lord,
> let the earth hear his voice!
> Praise the Lord, praise the Lord,
> let the people rejoice!
> O come to the Father thru Jesus the Son,
> and give him the glory, great things he hath done![7]

And of course, much of our sacramental theology points to substitutionary atonement by highlighting the role of Jesus's blood in bringing about the forgiveness of sins. In The United Methodist Church, when the presiding clergy lifts up the bread and the cup, they utter words that are directly drawn from both the Gospels and Paul, who understood the elements as a vivid reminder of Christ's sacrifice for us:

> On the night in which he gave himself up for us
>> he took bread, gave thanks to you, broke the bread,
>> gave it to his disciples, and said:
> "Take, eat; this is my body which is given for you.
> Do this in remembrance of me."

> When the supper was over, he took the cup,
>> gave thanks to you, gave it to his disciples,
>> and said:
> "Drink from this, all of you;
> this is my blood of the new covenant,
> poured out for you and for many
>> for the forgiveness of sins.
> Do this, as often as you drink it,
>> in remembrance of me.[8]

"KILLED IN A TRAITOR'S STEAD"

One of the great literary references to Christian substitutionary atonement is in *The Lion, the Witch and the Wardrobe*, the classic tale by C. S. Lewis. Its climactic scene contains a powerful and intentional allegory for the self-sacrificial work of Jesus. The enchanted world of Narnia had been cursed by the evil White Witch, who rendered the land a perpetual, snowy, and gloomy winter. She also enticed Edmund, one of the four child protagonists from the Pevensie family, to join her side.

After Edmund's siblings Lucy, Peter, and Susan successfully convinced Edmund of the White Witch's true evil ways, the White Witch declared Edmund a traitor, a sentence punishable only by death.

> "You at least know the Magic which the Emperor put into Narnia at the very beginning. You know that every traitor belongs to me as my lawful prey and that for every treachery I have a right to kill.... And so," continued the Witch, "that human creature is mine. His life is forfeit to me. His blood is my property.... unless I have blood as the Law says all Narnia will be overturned and perish in fire and water."

> "It is very true," said Aslan, "I do not deny it."[9]

In response, the great Aslan, a powerful kingly lion who had befriended the Pevensie children and whose presence threatened the power and reign of the White Witch, struck a deal with her. He would offer himself in the place of the traitor.

With the children secretly watching from a distance, the White Witch and her forces proceeded to torture and kill Aslan on the Stone Table, an act of self-sacrifice in which Aslan assumed the punishment on himself that had been intended for Edmund.

After his death, Aslan's body disappeared, leaving only a fractured Stone Table for the children to approach, grieving over the loss of their great friend. Then suddenly, a resurrected Aslan appeared before them, triumphant over death as well as the forces of the Witch.

When the puzzled children beckoned him for an explanation, Aslan offered some words that are an apt description of the power of substitutionary atonement theology:

"It means," said Aslan, "that though the Witch knew the Deep Magic, there is a magic deeper still which she did not know. Her knowledge goes back only to the dawn of time. But if she could have looked a little further back, into the stillness and the darkness before Time dawned, she would have read there a different incantation. She would have known that when a willing victim who had committed no treachery was killed in a traitor's stead, the Table would crack and Death itself would start working backward."[10]

This is the power of Christ's self-sacrifice. It calls us to name the unavoidable state of our guilt, because of the sins that sentence us to certain punishment. But it also reminds us that God in Christ has taken our place, assuming the painful price in his own body, so that the system of justice can be appeased, and our lives can be spared.

Jesus did for us what we could not do for ourselves. He, the "willing victim," was killed in our traitorous stead. And God did not give us what we deserved. That's the heart of substitutionary atonement.

> *Jesus did for us what we could not do for ourselves. He, the "willing victim," was killed in our traitorous stead. And God did not give us what we deserved. That's the heart of substitutionary atonement.*

THE LIMITATIONS OF SUBSTITUTIONARY ATONEMENT

Of course, substitutionary atonement has its detractors, and you might be one of them. No single image of how Christ's death brings about salvation is complete and all encompassing; every one of them has its shortcomings. It would be understandable if the imagery of bloody sacrifice simply doesn't resonate with you.

There are those who deem this idea as being far too antiquated, too distant from our contemporary worldview. We can be grateful that our legal system in particular, or our civic life together in general, does not require sacrifices in order to preserve order and decency. Especially in an age when there is far too much violence around us, and our news headlines and popular culture sometimes use bloodshed to sensationalize current events, many shun blood imagery as a reinforcement of our addictions to violence.

Despite the fact that many of our hymnals contain such titles as "There Is a Fountain Filled with Blood" and "There Is Power in the Blood," many people are simply turned off by such songs and what they deem to be too graphic for our modern sensibilities.

There is also a risk in misapplying this understanding of Christ's death. Because Jesus has taken our place and assumed the punishment we deserved, one might conclude that there is nothing more that we can or should do in response. In his book *The Great Omission*, author and theologian Dallas Willard used the label "vampire Christians" to describe followers of Jesus who are obsessed with blood atonement imagery, while failing to assume responsibility for their own diligent commitment to Christ.[11] They extract the personal benefit of Christ's blood sacrifice, without feeling the need to offer anything in return. The result can be a misguided portrait of the Christian life that demands little of our commitment because it required nothing of us for our salvation.

As we will discover in each of these chapters, each understanding of Christ's death has its merits as well as its limitations, and we can be free to extract the benefits of their rich traditions while acknowledging their drawbacks.

But for all the reservations one may have of substitutionary atonement, it does elicit one important response that is an important aspect of Christian character: Gratitude.

You and I can be grateful that Jesus did for us something that we could not do for ourselves, which we could not earn and did not deserve.

A RESPONSE OF GRATITUDE

Several years ago, when I was pastoring a church in Iowa, I learned quite an important lesson in a rather embarrassing way about grace and not getting what I deserved.

I had just finished making a pastoral visit on the south end of town when I stopped by a local gas station to pick up a bottle of iced tea before returning to the office. The attendant rang up my purchase, took a look at me, then paused.

He said to me, "You need to know that you drove off last week without paying for your gas."

"What?" I said, completely incredulous. "You're kidding! I did that?"

"Yes," he said. Apparently, at some point the prior week, I had come in, pumped gas, and then driven off without paying for it. He recognized both my face and my vehicle, and he was certain that it had been me.

I was absolutely shocked to hear the news. I had never pumped and ran in my life before (at least I don't think so!). And it was just not like me to even think about doing something like that. But I had no reason to disbelieve him, let alone try to prove him wrong. So, I started to pull my wallet out of my pocket when he said something that totally floored me.

"I just wanted you to know that I paid for your gas out of my own pocket."

I was stunned. I thanked him profusely. I stumbled over my words, overjoyed that he had not called the police, put the surveillance tapes on social media, or broadcast my deed to the local news. I quickly imagined what it would have been like for the town newspaper to lead with the headline, "Local United Methodist Pastor Becomes Thief."

I thanked him again. And again.

"It's okay," he told me. "I knew you would be back here someday for me to tell you. So I covered you."

I walked away from that conversation feeling the most sheepish I'd felt in a long time. But I was also filled with immense gratitude. I had not gotten what I deserved. And this man had given me something I could not earn.

Looking back at that event now, I can make lots of theological connections to substitutionary atonement. For all of its blood imagery and graphic violence, this understanding of Christ's death elicits a singularly pure response: a feeling of gratitude, recognizing that God has done something so amazing for us.

In Christ, God gave us something we didn't deserve and didn't give us the punishment we should have received. Instead, Christ himself assumed our punishment, "covered us," in a sense, much like that gracious gas station attendant did for me.

And what's more, the gas station attendant didn't even ask me to pay him back. As much as I tried, he told me not to bother. Perhaps it was because it was not worth his trouble to look back at the old purchases. Perhaps it was because this was a small Midwestern town, and people just kind of look out for each other when they mess up.

Ultimately, I think it was because of the generosity of the attendant himself, who knew that someone had to take the fall for my mistake, and he was willing to do it himself.

The only response to that is sheer, unbridled gratitude.

It's true that substitutionary atonement has its drawbacks. None of these approaches to the cross are perfect, which is why there are so many in Scripture and in the traditions in the church throughout our history. But this idea does succeed in eliciting the kind of grateful response to God that I think we need to express more often.

It is captured beautifully in the hymn by Charles Wesley, "And Can It Be that I Should Gain."

> And can it be that I should gain an interest in the Savior's blood!
>
> Died he for me? who caused his pain! For me? who him to death pursued?
>
> Amazing love! How can it be that thou, my God, shouldst die for me?
>
> Amazing love! How can it be that thou, my God, shouldst die for me?

20

SUBSTITUTIONARY ATONEMENT IN SUMMARY

Definition of Sin: Sin is a violation of God's intended order for creation and violates the very nature of God. We owe an infinite debt for this violation and, therefore, deserve punishment for our sin.

Definition of Salvation: Jesus died in our place, repaying our debt, so that we don't have to.

Pros: Substitutionary atonement is rooted in numerous biblical passages and has been an important part of the Christian tradition for many centuries.

Cons: Blood imagery contradicts our modern sensibilities and can feed our culture's addiction to violence. It can lead us to follow Christ passively rather than actively.

Response: Substitutionary atonement can elicit a deep sense of gratitude to God, that Jesus did for us that which we could not do for ourselves.

REFLECTING ON THE CROSS

When was there a time that someone did something for you that you could not do for yourself?

What are your impressions of substitutionary atonement? What do you find appealing? And what do you struggle with?

How might you live with greater gratitude for what Jesus did for you?

CHAPTER 2

RANSOM:
JESUS SETS
YOU FREE

CHAPTER 2

RANSOM:
JESUS SETS YOU FREE

Luke 4:16-30 • Acts 16:16-29

There is nothing about the term *ransom* that is to be taken lightly. It has connotations of captivity and bondage and the desperate means that the victim will go to secure freedom. When you think of *ransom*, you might think of a ransom note—harrowing correspondence from a captor, and the attempt to extract some kind of gain for the release of the captive.

There is nothing fun about it.

Yet, if you think of it, we do embed into many of our childhood games some form of captivity and release. I remember the glee that my friends and I would feel when we reported to elementary school gym class and heard from the coach that we would be playing dodgeball that day. The goal of dodgeball was pretty simple. Take one of those large red rubbery playground balls, throw them across the court, and hit the other kids without getting hit. If you got hit, you were out, and you were relegated to some area outside the playing field to wait and mope. Basically, you were put in "jail," as my friends and I called it. (I'm not sure if that was the official term, but calling it that added to the misery of being out.)

It wouldn't be until another player on your team bravely and skillfully stepped up, amid the flying fury of playground projectiles, and successfully caught one of the other team's throws, that you had the possibility of being sprung loose, free to reenter the game and rejoin your teammates. That was always a thrill for me, because I was in dodgeball jail quite often.

Dodgeball is not the only game like that. Think about the "mush pot" in Duck Duck Goose where you'd have to sit until the next victim took your place. Or the jail in Kick the Can where you would be sentenced once you were tagged, and would remain until an untagged friend kicked the can over. Or the "Go to Jail" card in Monopoly, where you would spend endless turns as one passerby after another turned the corner and gawked at you on their way around the board.

Captivity is no fun, even in a children's game.

One biblical view of what Jesus accomplished on the cross is built on the idea that sin has held us hostage, imprisoned by a captor who is beyond our control. That sin binds our abilities to live the free and forgiven life that God intends for us. We are prisoners of the forces of evil and wickedness, and there is no hope for escape on our own efforts. In this view, Jesus saves us by giving his life on the cross as a ransom to set us free.

> *We are prisoners of the forces of evil and wickedness, and there is no hope for escape on our own efforts.*

RANSOM ATONEMENT
IN THE BIBLE AND HISTORY

About a hundred years after Jesus, a man named Irenaeus first began to think about the problem of the human condition as one of being held captive by sin and evil in the world. He was compelled by the imagery of captivity, and he gave our kidnapper a name as "the apostate one," or the devil. Here is how he described the way the devil holds people captive in their sins:

> The apostate one (or, the devil) unjustly held sway over us, and though we were by nature the possession of Almighty God, we had been alienated from our proper nature, making us instead his own disciples.[1]

In other words, we were kidnapped, sent to dodgeball jail, put in the mush pot. Or, to use words that acknowledge the severity of our captivity, we were enslaved in chains. We were stolen away from the kind of life that we were created to live, swept away from the joy, peace, and love that was supposed to characterize our existence. And we could not escape on our own.

Many centuries later, Thomas Cranmer (1489–1556), the Archbishop of Canterbury, developed this image further, describing Christ's body and blood as a price that God had to negotiate with the devil and pay in full in order to extract our freedom:

> Whereas all the world was not able of themselves to pay any part towards their ransom, it pleased our heavenly Father of his infinite mercy, without any our desert or deserving, to prepare for us the most precious jewels of Christ's body and blood, whereby our

ransom might be fully paid, the law fulfilled, and his justice fully satisfied.[2]

Both Cranmer and Irenaeus based their ideas largely on the words of the apostle Paul, who often used the imagery of chains to describe not just his physical imprisonment, but the bondage of sin that holds us hostage.

> *Now before faith came, we were imprisoned and guarded under the law until faith would be revealed. Therefore the law was our disciplinarian until Christ came, so that we might be justified by faith. But now that faith has come, we are no longer subject to a disciplinarian, for in Christ Jesus you are all children of God through faith.*
>
> *(Galatians 3:23-26 NRSV)*

Irenaeus also drew from the words of Jesus, particularly from his famous first sermon in Luke 4. In it, Jesus ushered in his public ministry by declaring his personal mission statement to the word: he has come to set free those who are held in bondage to sin:

> *[The Lord] has sent me to preach good news to the poor,*
> *to proclaim release to the prisoners*
> *and recovery of sight to the blind,*
> *to liberate the oppressed (v. 18).*

FREEDOM FOR THE OPPRESSED

In this notion of a Jesus who sides with the captives, we see the profound power of an approach to Jesus's work on the cross that emphasizes ransom. It points to the full extent of the freedom Jesus

28

offers us. Jesus frees us not only from the spiritual bondage of sin, but from all other forms of bondage that stem from it—economic, political, and cultural captivity. For those who are marginalized and oppressed in any way, Jesus comes to set them free.

> *Jesus frees us not only from the spiritual bondage of sin, but from all other forms of bondage that stem from it—economic, political, and cultural captivity.*

George Johnson, former director of the world hunger program for the American Lutheran Church and author of *Beyond Guilt and Powerlessness*, said that Luke 4:16-30 and the image of salvation as being set free from captivity, is the heart of the gospel for many Latin American countries.

He reminds us that in this country, our favorite "gospel in a nutshell" Bible verse is John 3:16: "For God so loved the world, that he gave his only begotten Son, that whosoever believeth in him should not perish, but have everlasting life" (KJV). He said that the ultimate goal for many Christians in America is eternal, everlasting life. It's such a popular image for salvation that we see "John 3:16" inscribed everywhere, from t-shirts to stadium signs.

But not so in many Latin American countries. There it is not John 3:16 that summarizes salvation, but Luke 4:16-30. Salvation in that context is about "good news to the poor," "release to the captives," "recovery of sight to the blind," and "freedom for those who are oppressed."[3]

The biblical imagery of ransom therefore supports one of the most powerful contemporary theological movements in the church, which is liberation theology. This includes Latin American liberation theology by theologians such as Gustavo Gutiérrez in the Roman Catholic Church in the 1950s and 60s, for the countries of Peru, Brazil, and Ecuador. And it includes Black liberation theology in this country, with theologians such as James Cone talking about the African-American experience. Liberation theology centers on the idea that God is always on the side of the oppressed, never the oppressor and that God's justice will ultimately come down to set free those who are imprisoned by the spiritual, economic, and societal forces that are holding us back.

A story is told by noted child psychiatrist Dr. Robert Coles about a conversation he had with a young girl who was part of a migrant farmworker family.

He asked the little girl to draw pictures of herself and various people she knew—her family members, friends, and the owner of the land the girl and her family worked, whom she called the "bossman." She drew each one, but drew the "bossman" a little differently than the rest. He was off in the distance, away from the field, and finely dressed. But most curiously, this figure unlike the others was looking up into the sky, with arms and palms extended. His upward gaze caught Coles's attention.

"What is the bossman doing?"

"He is looking up for God," the little girl replied.

When asked why, she said, "He wants to make sure God is on his side. The minister says Jesus was on the side of the poor, so that could mean trouble for him [the bossman], and he's trying to avoid that, getting himself on the wrong side of the Lord, because that can mean big, big trouble."[4]

SETTING YOU FREE

The idea of ransom, of release of those who are captive, has certainly shaken up systems of cultural, political, and economic oppression. But it is also powerful on a personal level. Many have drawn strength from this understanding of Jesus's death after identifying the many ways that they feel held hostage by forces beyond their control.

It would be worth pondering how you feel like you are in bondage within your own life. From what chains do you need to be freed?

Maybe yours is a chain of addiction. Maybe there are those lingering, pestering habitual temptations in your life that have festered for many, many years. Maybe your self-destructive behavior has cost you in relationships, means, and hopes.

Maybe your chain is one of guilt. Maybe you are daily haunted by mistakes from your past. Maybe you have never truly experienced the forgiveness of God, and certainly never practiced forgiveness of yourself. Maybe you can't look in the mirror in the morning without hanging your head and drooping your spirit. Shame and guilt is one of the Christian's deadliest enemies, and Christ has come to set you free of that.

Maybe your chain today is one of hopelessness in a cruel, perverse world. Maybe you can't read the newspaper without feeling utter grief over the state of the world. Innocent people suffering, unsuspecting people dying, diseases running rampant, global uncertainties, countries at war.

Maybe your chain is one of anger, bitterness, or resentment. Maybe you have long held on to deep wounds created by the betrayal of another person. Maybe you still can't let go of the feelings of vindication or revenge associated with past hurts.

Maybe your chain is one of sincere and skeptical doubt about your Christian experience. Maybe you have a sense at times that God is not fully present with you or that you do not feel the full depth of relationship with Christ that you ought.

Maybe your chain is the fear of death.

Maybe your chain is anxiety about your future.

Maybe your chain is one of disease.

If any of these images of chains sound like a good metaphor for the struggles you are facing in your life, then the cross of Jesus Christ offers you this good news. Jesus has come to set you free. He has paid your ransom, guaranteed your release. What has held you back need not hold you back any longer.

> *Jesus has come to set you free. He has paid your ransom, guaranteed your release. What has held you back need not hold you back any longer.*

And even after we have been set free, Paul would remind us that those moments of captivity in our past can make us even more grateful for the freedom we might experience now or down the road. "Remember my chains," Paul tells Christians in Colossians 4:18 (NRSV). While the memories of our past difficulties never go away, they can remind us of how God still has the power to liberate us and make us grateful for every moment, one day at a time.

PROS AND CONS OF RANSOM ATONEMENT THEORY

As is the case for each image of how Jesus's death saves us, the ransom metaphor has its drawbacks as well as its advantages. Some find problematic the implicit suggestion that the world is dualistic in nature, in which God has a cosmically powerful foe in the universe like Satan or the devil, who can hold us hostage despite God's desire to prevent it. Some versions of the ransom theory suggest that the devil is able to negotiate with God for our release, which is an uncomfortable way of looking at the work of Jesus and might call God's omnipotence into question.

The focus on sin as captivity can also remove agency from human beings to be the cause of their own sins. It isn't our fault we are sinful, this theory might suggest, for, in the words of comedian Flip Wilson, "The devil made [us] do it."

Despite these shortcomings, there are certainly advantages to describing our salvation in terms of ransom as well. For one thing, this image takes seriously the power of sin and reminds us that on our own accord we can't break ourselves free. That's a good reminder, especially in a culture that would have us believe that, with enough self-actualization and positive pep talk, we can overcome any obstacle and be anything we want to be. That's true in some ways but not in everything. There are some chains that are simply too hard for us to break on our own.

The ransom image is so prominent in the Bible and throughout Christian history that it is comforting to think that we are not alone whenever we feel powerless against sin and suffering. Others have endured the hardship and experienced Christ's freedom, and we can too.

And that is something to sing about!

SINGING IN CAPTIVITY

Throughout the Bible, when people were being held captive, they discovered music as a way of claiming their freedom. And

33

when they were released from captivity, they could not help but raise their voice in jubilant song.

One of the earliest Scripture passages ever written, according to biblical scholars, was "The Song of the Sea" in Exodus 15. Moses and his sister Miriam led the Israelites in song after the Israelites crossed through the Red Sea and escaped Pharaoh's army.

Centuries later, the Israelite kingdom would fall at the hands of the Assyrian and Babylonian empires. Jerusalem would crumble, and great buildings would lie in ruins, including the once proud and beautiful temple. Most of its citizens were dragged into captivity in Babylon, wondering how they might sing the songs of old in a foreign land (Psalm 137:4). Yet in Isaiah 52, they find their voice to sing, not just songs of lament, but songs of joy. They sing with the conviction that God would rebuild both the city of Jerusalem and the hearts of the people.

And when Mary learned that she would give birth to a child who would enter a world overrun by the proud and the powerful, she broke into the Magnificat, a song that proclaims favor for the lowly and the oppressed.

These are all great examples of singing in solitude and singing in suffering—Miriam, Mary, the exiles—but one of the most vivid examples of how to claim God's freedom in the midst of captivity is in the Book of Acts, where we find Paul and Silas.

In Acts 16, Paul and Silas were in prison for disturbing the peace in Philippi. They sat in the dark of midnight behind bars, sore and bruised from the brutal flogging administered by their captors. Yet what is it they were doing as they prayed in that dark and awful imprisonment?

Singing praise to God. What a remarkable thing to do.

Acts doesn't tell us what song they were singing. The only early church hymn that we know is from Philippians 2, which had not been written yet. They could have been singing Psalms, set to familiar tunes. We don't know. For all we know, they could have been making it up as they went.

Nor do we know how well they were singing, which ought to be of great comfort to those who feel like they can't carry a tune in a bucket. Besides, when they sang, their pitch and intonation were drowned out by an earthquake so massive that it shook the jail and caused the prison doors to fly open. It's not about what song you sing or how you sing it. It's about the power of God that you claim in the midst of your captivity that makes all the difference.

When you are in distress, find your song.

SINGING OUT IN FREEDOM

It should be no surprise, then, that the ransom idea of atonement has inspired some of our most popular and most cherished hymns, including the well-known Advent hymn "O Come, O Come Emmanuel":

> O come, O come, Emmanuel,
> and ransom captive Israel,
> that mourns in lonely exile here
> until the Son of God appear.
>
> Rejoice! Rejoice! Emmanuel
> shall come to thee, O Israel.

Some versions of the hymn include this verse, which also alludes to the ransom idea:

O come, Thou Rod of Jesse, free
Thine own from Satan's tyranny;
From depths of hell Thy people save,
And give them victory o'er the grave.

Then there is "O For a Thousand Tongues to Sing," one of the most famous hymns written by Charles Wesley, who succinctly and powerfully describes how Jesus "breaks the power of canceled sin; he sets the prisoner free."

Both of these hymns, and many others anchored in the idea of ransom, remind us that in Christ, we can not only be set free *from* our imprisonment; we can even experience freedom *during* our imprisonment.

And just as Wesley's hymn suggests, one of the ways to claim that freedom is through song.

The great composer Steven Sondheim said, "If I cannot fly, let me sing."[5] Indeed, in those moments when we feel most bound, most shackled, most limited to our earthen, human condition—in those moments when we feel most imprisoned—sometimes, the way to rise and fly above it is to sing a song of freedom and confidence in the power of God.

That was certainly the case for black slaves in the nineteenth century, who sang the African-American spirituals as a way of claiming their hope in God in the midst of their struggle. That's the way it was during the civil rights era, when songs like "We Shall Overcome" and "Lift Every Voice and Sing" became the songs of freedom from oppression.

When John Wesley was caught in a tumultuous storm in the middle of the Atlantic Ocean early in his ministry career as he was on his way to serve as a missionary in Georgia, he looked at a group of fellow Christians—Moravians—who were singing in the midst of the storm. And it was their peace that made Wesley crave an assurance for his salvation.

One time, during a particularly tough stretch of my life and ministry, I paid a visit to my therapist, who always had a way of listening to the deepest stirrings of my heart and offering just the right words of encouragement and truth telling when I needed it most.

In that session, my therapist, knowing what I did for a living, suggested, "How about turning on a Christian radio station?"

That suggestion surprised me. She and I had never really talked about music before, and I had to admit to her in that moment that I had had kind of an on-again, off-again relationship with Christian music. There were times earlier in my life when that was all I listened to. At other times, I listened to less of it, as I diversified my taste in music.

But she made a good case. "I'm a firm believer that if you fill your mind with positive things," she explained, "then that reduces the room for the negative,"

Later that week, driving back to the church after a lunch meeting, feeling particularly down-and-out about a number of things, I remembered her suggestion, and I checked out the local Christian radio station.

The song "Blessings" by Laura Story came on, and her lyrics washed over me like a salve on a harsh wound.[6]

> 'Cause what if your blessings come through raindrops?
> What if Your healing comes through tears?

As I neared the church office, I pulled the car over, listening to the whole song as she described sleepless nights and trials as a means God can use to reach us. I was assured that God was with me, amid the heartache and suffering of the moment.

Is that what Miriam, Mary, the exiles, and Paul and Silas were experiencing as they sang in their captivity? Is that what you can experience when you claim the salvation of Jesus who comes to set us free?

It sure sounds like it to me. There is power in singing songs while you are in solitude.

One of my favorite things to do when I go out for pastoral visits, particularly people in the hospital or in care facilities, is to bring my hymnal. I started doing this when I first became a minister many years ago, for a few reasons. First, when I walk into a hospital with my hymnal, it gives a pretty clear visual signal that I'm a pastor. Rather than flash a badge or present a business card, showing my hymnal is often enough of an indication that I'm there to do ministry.

Mostly, I bring a hymnal because one of my favorite questions to ask an older patient or parishioner is what song they want to hear during their hour of need. I find that the hymn they select for me to sing can be just as revealing about their state of mind or their emotional being or their history in the faith as any direct question I can ask them. Sometimes they will tell me a hymn that their mother used to sing to them. Or they will tell me a hymn that was sung at their loved one's funeral. Or they will simply tell me one that has been meaningful to them along the journey of their life.

And then, it never ceases to amaze me what can happen as I am singing their hymn.

Many Alzheimer's patients that I've visited will begin to sing along or mouth the lyrics, remembering little else but the words to that hymn. People in the hospital will begin to tear up as they hear their emotions lifted up in song.

It's never about my singing. I know that. Rather, what happens in those moments is that they begin to fly, as Sondheim said. There, in the confines of their ill health, in the imprisonment of their earthly bodies and broken lives, they begin to see through the power of song the possibility of freedom. And that freedom leads them to hope and hope brings them joy and joy brings them new life in the midst of darkness.

In other words, like Paul and Silas, they feel an earthquake-sized stirring in their souls, even in the midst of their captivity.

In May 1984, Presbyterian missionaries Ben and Carol Weir were taken hostage in Beirut, Lebanon, along with several other Americans. For sixteen long months, the hostages spent most of the time in isolation, except for their captors, chained to radiators in small rooms of buildings in Lebanon. They were blindfolded much of the time and beaten on occasion. They were never sure, as the days turned into weeks and then months, whether they would live to see family and friends and freedom again.

One day early in his captivity, Ben Weir began to imagine that it was dusk outside and began picturing in his mind the beauty of the setting sun. As he did so, a hymn came to mind: "Abide with me; fast falls the eventide." In that moment of vulnerability, loneliness, and helplessness, tears came to his eyes, as he remembered the promise of Jesus—that he would be with us always. Soon Ben thought of another evening hymn: "All Praise to Thee, My God, This Night..." He found that his tears were then prompted by gratitude and a sense of companionship and intimacy.

39

In his memoir *Hostage Bound, Hostage Free*, Ben wrote: "As darkness became complete, I found myself recalling one hymn after another. Of some I could remember several verses, and where there was a gap I could improvise. Of others I could only remember a phrase or two. I was surprised to see how many came to mind."[7] He sang the great historical hymns of the church. He sang gospel tunes and children's songs and Christmas carols and Easter hymns. For Ben, each hymn communicated some aspect of the Christian life and faith that were meaningful to him.

The feeling of imprisonment is disheartening, especially when it comes to sins that feel like shackles on your spirit. It can feel dire and desperate, as you acknowledge how powerless you are to break the chains that prevent you from living the full and free life that God wants for you. It is just as unsettling when you see loved ones struggle time and again with bonds that seem unbreakable.

But God has come to us in Jesus, who "breaks the power of canceled sin, and sets the prisoner free." Believing that power means claiming our voice and finding our song, which enables us to acknowledge God's incessant love for us.

May the fourth stanza of Charles Wesley's hymn "And Can It Be that I Should Gain" remind you of that love, and prompt you to be grateful, no matter your circumstances.

> Long my imprisoned spirit lay,
> fast bound in sin and nature's night;
> thine eye diffused a quickening ray;
> I woke, the dungeon flamed with light;
> my chains fell off, my heart was free,
> I rose, went forth, and followed thee.
> My chains fell off, my heart was free,
> I rose, went forth, and followed thee.

RANSOM ATONEMENT IN SUMMARY

Definition of Sin: Sin holds us hostage, preventing us from living the kind of life that God intends for us to live.

Definition of Salvation: Jesus pays our ransom and sets us free, releasing us from captivity and enabling us to live in freedom and joy.

Pros: It takes sin seriously and reminds us that we cannot break free on our own. There is comfort and power in the notion that God is on the side of the oppressed, and those held in spiritual, economic, political, and cultural captivity can be liberated by the power and grace of God.

Cons: Can be seen as being built on a dualistic worldview, in which good and evil are at equal odds with each other.

Response: Because Jesus has set us free, it is now incumbent on us to act like we are free and not take advantage of our freedom by continuing to live in sin.

REFLECTING ON THE CROSS

In what ways are you being held captive by sin, and by forces that seem beyond your control?

Who in your community lives in economic, political, and cultural captivity? How might your efforts as a follower of Jesus contribute to their liberation?

How will your freedom in Christ help you find your song?

CHAPTER 3

MORAL EXAMPLE: JESUS SHOWS YOU HOW TO LIVE

CHAPTER 3

1 John 3:11-24 * Matthew 5–7

MORAL EXAMPLE:
JESUS SHOWS YOU
HOW TO LIVE

In the second season of the children's television program *The New Adventures of Winnie the Pooh* was an episode titled "Un-Valentine's Day." It began with a meeting in Rabbit's house, filled with the whole beloved population of the Hundred Acre Wood. They had gathered to discuss the fallout from the previous year's Valentine's Day, in which the card giving and gift sharing had gotten so out of hand that "ten zillion" cards flooded into everyone's homes, to the point that they could not even see their houses. A day designated to celebrate and demonstrate love became cheapened by competition and one-upmanship.

That left Rabbit to make this proclamation: Valentine's Day would be canceled in the Hundred Acre Wood. They had failed to fully live into the spirit of the day, to love each other, turning it into something more self-serving than self-sacrificial, and it was undermining their connection to each other.

But eventually, the story took a turn for the better.

After Rabbit declared an end to Valentine's Day and banned all giving and receiving of cards and notes, Pooh woke up the next morning and saw a honey-pot sitting on his front step. Pooh liked honey very much. He ate it right up, and he realized that such a wonderful gift of love must have come from his friend Piglet. Overcome with gratitude, Pooh decided to share that love with Piglet in the form of a pot full of honey. (Of course, true to Pooh's character, by the time he got to Piglet, the pot was half full of honey! But it was the thought that counted.)

You can then guess what happened next. One by one, each character in the Hundred Acre Wood was so overcome by these acts of love that they started giving gifts to each other. Piglet made a cake and delivered it to Owl, who then gave Tigger a gift, and so forth down the line until Rabbit received an anonymous, gift-wrapped carrot.

All because one person decided to model love for everyone in the Wood to follow.

That person, as it turned out, was Christopher Robin, their benevolent companion and bridge to a life beyond the Hundred Acre Wood. Christopher never had bought into Rabbit's notion of an Un-Valentine's Day, choosing instead to break through the silliness by showing them how to love each other.

MORAL EXAMPLE ATONEMENT THEORY

The Moral Example (or Moral Influence) understanding of how Jesus saves us is based on an understanding of sin in which we have taken the gift of God's love and corrupted it, turning every day into an "Un-Valentine's Day." But through the example of Jesus's life, teachings, death, and resurrection, he shows us how to live, how to love, and how to be in full relationship with God and one another.

It begins with a fundamental reminder of the original nature of human beings, which is that we are created in the image of God. That is what we first learn about human beings in the Book of Genesis. Our creation in God's image means that in our essence we have the capacity and potential to reflect God's love into the world. It does not mean that we are God, or equal with God, but that we are God's "imprint." It means that God's basic character of goodness, love, and relationality is an integral part of who we are created to be.

> *God's basic character of goodness, love, and relationality is an integral part of who we are created to be.*

Then, just like what happened in the Hundred Acre Wood, the garden of Eden became a place where humans took that gift of love and made it self-centered, competitive, divisive. That image of God within us became so tarnished, tainted, and diminished that humans have fallen, and continue to fall, far short of being able to reflect God's love into the world.

That reality is the essence of how the Moral Example approach to atonement understands sin. Unlike substitutionary atonement, where sin is defined as an action punishable by death, or the ransom concept, in which sin is an imprisonment we cannot escape, or the upcoming approaches that describe sin in other ways, the Moral

Example perspective defines sin as our inability to fully reflect the image of God in and through our lives.

In a sense, that makes every day an Un-Valentine's Day.

And what we need to restore this world back to its intended order is someone to show us the way of love again. Someone to model for us what a full image of God looks like again. And someone to empower us to follow that example in the way we live, act, think, and relate to others.

Someone even better than Christopher Robin. A person named Jesus Christ.

"This is how we know love," we read in John's first epistle. "Jesus laid down his life for us, and we ought to lay down our lives for our brothers and sister.... Little children, let's not love with words or speech but with action and truth" (vv. 3:16, 18).

MORAL EXAMPLE IN HISTORY

This way of understanding the significance of Jesus's death may sound new and unfamiliar, but it has actually been around for hundreds of years. In fact, aspects of it can be traced all the way back to the first centuries of the church, as they were taught by early thinkers like Iraneaus, Polycarp, Ignatius, Origen, and Clement. We can see its roots in some of the earliest Christian documents, like the *Didache* and the *Shepherd of Hermas* (Christian texts that did not become a part of the Bible but were well known and influential in the early church).

Despite these forerunners, the moral example idea was not articulated in a single theological framework until a French philosopher named Peter Abelard came along in the twelfth century. He helped usher it into more widespread recognition by giving it a formal, clear expression, even as Christian understanding of Jesus's death was replete with more popular ideas like substitutionary atonement. Abelard said:

> Now it seems to us that we have been justified by the blood of Christ and reconciled to God in this way: through this unique act of grace manifested to us— in that his Son has taken upon himself our nature and persevered therein in teaching us by word and example even unto death…he has more fully bound us to himself by love; with the result that our hearts should be enkindled by such a gift of divine grace, and true charity should not now shrink from enduring anything for him…so that we do all things out of love rather than fear.[1]

Abelard affirmed other atonement concepts like substitution ("justified by the blood of Christ") and reconciliation ("and reconciled to God in this way"). But he also understood that the present nature of human beings is characterized by an inability to fully reflect God's image created in us. So, Jesus "persevered therein in teaching us by word and example" how to reveal that image for others and be the people of love that God intended for us to be. Part of the example that Jesus set for us is his willingness to surrender himself to death on the cross, the ultimate act of self-giving love, showing us that we should "do all things out of love rather than fear."

The ultimate outcome of salvation, then, according to Abelard's Moral Example understanding, is that we become more able to love the way God loves, to forgive the way God forgives, to be in fuller and holier relationships with others, to be better stewards of creation, and to seek the way of humble service.

> *e ultimate outcome of salvation is that*
> *we become more able to love the way God*
> *loves, to forgive the way God forgives, to*
> *be in fuller and holier relationships with*
> *others, to be better stewards of creation,*
> *and to seek the way of humble service.*

It becomes fairly evident that what sets this idea apart from the other approaches to atonement is that it does not locate salvation exclusively on Jesus's death on the cross. The entirety of Jesus's life is what constitutes salvation for us. His life, his teachings, his actions, his suffering, his death, and his resurrection: all of it was important to save us.

THE PROS AND CONS OF THE MORAL EXAMPLE THEORY

The Moral Example idea also helps answer some potentially tricky questions. Questions like, "What if, instead of dying at the age of thirty-three, after three years of public ministry and teaching, he had died at, say, the age of twenty? Before he did any work as the Messiah? Would he still have been our Savior?"

By focusing on Jesus's role as an example for us to follow, an approach like Abelard's would suggest the answer is no, because it was not just the cross, but Christ's teaching and example that show us how to live that saves us. If he had died on the cross at twenty, then we wouldn't have the fully divine example to follow, and we would still have that tarnished image of God affecting us.

And, what would have happened if, instead of dying on a cross, Jesus had died a natural death, like dying of old age or disease or a heart attack and then three days later coming back from the dead? Would his actions still have saved us?

Again this approach would answer no, not because it needs spilled blood or the gore of the Crucifixion, but because in the cross, Jesus demonstrated for us the greatest quality that we need to have in order to fully reveal God's image in us. It's the quality of love. Genuine, self-emptying, self-sacrificial love. The kind of love that would lead us to lay down our lives selflessly for the benefit of others.

There are many reasons people find the Moral Example theory of the atonement to be appealing. First, like all the other approaches, it is grounded in Scripture. One of the many running themes throughout the Gospels and the letters of Paul is how to live the moral, righteous, godly life. The greatest sermon Jesus preached, the Sermon on the Mount, is almost entirely focused on living a holy life, in direct contrast to our inner urges and the pressures of the culture. The letters of Paul to the churches contain countless instructions on how the people of God are to behave as individuals and in community together and in mission to the world. The New Testament, as well as much of the Hebrew Bible, cares a great deal about how close you live your life to the standards that God has for you and how you can live up to your potential.

First John 3 is also very clear: if you want to reveal the image of God, the potential God has given you, then your utmost concern should be love.

To love one another, to forgive without holding a grudge.
To seek peace, not violence or hatred.
To care for the outcast and the oppressed.

And if you want an example of that, then look at Jesus. His example saves you. "This is his commandment," John says, "that we believe in the name of his Son, Jesus Christ, and love each other as he commanded us" (1 John 3:23)

Another advantage of the Moral Example understanding is its concern about the here and now, rather than solely focusing on the future. Some tend to fixate on the idea that the goal of the Christian life is entirely about getting to heaven, as if all that really matters about being a Christian is where we go after we die. Heaven or hell, eternal reward or eternal damnation?

The Moral Example concept would remind us that Jesus spent a lot less time in his public ministry talking about life after death and a whole lot more time encouraging people to live out the kingdom of God right here and right now. He even said it in the way he modeled prayer for his disciples: "Your kingdom come…on earth as it is in heaven" (Matthew 6:10 NRSV). And he said, "I am with you always, to the end of the age" (Matthew 28:20 NRSV). In other words, he told his followers not to live their lives in expectation of his coming back someday, because he would always be with them, right here, right now, all the time. It is the present that really matters.

This theory reminds us that the goal of the Christian life is how we live today, how we love, act, serve, and seek justice, compassion, and holiness.

It is about how well we live out the image of God within us and for others, following the example of Jesus Christ.

There are certainly some drawbacks to the Moral Example concept as well. Because much of it is about what we do here on earth, critics claim that it is much too dependent on our works, rather than on the gift of God's grace. And that, of course, flies in the face of one of our chief tenets as Christians. So, an emphasis on Jesus as a moral example for us to follow needs to be supplemented with an equally strong conviction about God's grace. It is only by God's grace that we have the ability to discern Christ's example and the strength to follow it. John Wesley would call this the sanctifying grace of God, which helps us on a daily basis take the actions necessary to live as Christ.

Another disadvantage for some is that the theory seems to minimize the work of the cross. If you're someone who needs the central image of the Crucifixion, the blood, the nail scars, and the death of Jesus, then another atonement theory might be more suitable for you.

Ultimately, there are many who find this theory appealing because it counters the notion that violence brings salvation. In a world where violence and aggression seem to be the default response in solving personal and international problems, this theory suggests that it's not the way of bloodshed and violence, but the way of self-sacrifice and self-giving that is the way to true salvation.

And when I think of the power of nonviolence to offer salvation for the world, one of the people I think of is Óscar Romero.

SELF-GIVING LOVE

Óscar Romero was a Roman Catholic archbishop who lived in El Salvador in the twentieth century. His advocacy for the marginalized and oppressed often put him at odds with both the government and the hierarchy of the Roman Catholic Church. After speaking out against US military support for the Salvadoran government and calling for soldiers to disobey orders that harmed human rights, Romero was shot to death while celebrating Mass at a small chapel near his cathedral. It is believed that his assassins were members of Salvadoran death squads.

During that final, fateful Eucharistic service, Romero spoke these hauntingly prescient words: "May this body immolated and this blood sacrificed for humans nourish us also, so that we may give our body and our blood to suffer and to pain—like Christ, not for self, but to bring about justice and peace for our people." Romero believed that being a Christian means much more than pious platitudes and emotional ego-stroking. It beckons us to model our lives after the example of Christ's self-giving, self-sacrificial love. He believed that our lives needed to echo Christ's compassion for the poor, the exploited, and the suffering among us.[2]

Yet, his advocacy never involved violence. In a time when our news headlines are filled with more warfare than peacemaking, when tyrants brutalize their own citizens, and as our already taxed military enters its third international engagement, Romero's words are a clarion call for the Kingdom value of nonviolence. "We have never preached violence," he said, "except the violence of love, which left Christ nailed to a cross, the violence that we must each do to ourselves to overcome our selfishness and such cruel inequalities among us. The violence we preach is not the violence of the sword, the violence of hatred. It is the violence of love, of brotherhood, the violence that wills to beat weapons into sickles for work."[3]

Romero also felt that: "One must not love oneself so much, as to avoid getting involved in the risks of life that history demands of us, and those who try to fend off danger will lose their lives." Just a short time later, with a single sniper's bullet to the heart, Romero collapsed to the ground behind the altar, the shadow of the crucified Christ looming behind him. His blood spilt onto the ground, a stirring symbol of a man who followed the example of Christ in every way possible.

The question for us today is whether we are willing to accept the example that Jesus laid down for us. For if we can, by the strength and power of the Spirit, follow that example, we can live the life God has intended for us to live. Not just into the future, after we die, but here and now. For the benefit of the world and for the sake of the cross.

It is a question asked by composer Earl Marlatt, whose hymn "Are Ye Able" captures the gravity of following Jesus, all the way to the cross:

> "Are ye able," said the Master,
> "to be crucified with me?"
> "Yea," the sturdy dreamers answered,
> "to the death we follow thee."
>
> Lord, we are able. Our spirits are thine.
> Remold them, make us, like thee, divine.
> Thy guiding radiance above us shall be
> a beacon to God, to love, and loyalty.

THE DIFFICULT WAY OF LOVE

The challenge, of course, is that following the example of Jesus is hard! Despite what Marlatt's hymn says, we can readily admit our reluctance to be crucified with Jesus. We find ourselves quite set in our ways, comfortable in the perspectives, routines, and behaviors that govern our interactions with God and others.

But Jesus knew that sometimes the most important lessons we need to hear are not the ones we want to hear, but Jesus would offer them with direct honesty. They are found throughout the Gospels, and we might categorize them as "Things that we wish Jesus had never said, but that we need to hear."

The following is by no means a comprehensive list, but it is enough to cover the range of some of the most difficult teachings Jesus offered in the Gospels. Some you might find to be easy. Others of them (most of them, perhaps) are ones that you need to hear, but are reluctant to apply:

Love your enemies. We'll just start right out of the gate with what may be the toughest one of them all, right? I mean, c'mon Jesus. We'd rather eat our vegetables than follow this lesson. But Jesus said it pretty clearly in Matthew 5:43-44: "You have heard that it was said, *You must love your neighbor* and hate your enemy. But I say to you, love your enemies and pray for those who harass you." And I can hear the five-year old kid inside each one of us saying to God the same line we used to say to our parents when we were kids:

"Do we really have to?" Yes, Jesus says. We really have to.

God or money. Choose. Jesus never said there was anything wrong with earning money, saving money, or spending money. He never said there was anything wrong with having money. But in Matthew 6:24, he basically says, "You cannot serve God and wealth." In other words, you cannot worship money. Not if you want to worship God. You cannot obsess over it or let it control you. And the same goes for your possessions, your investments, and your public image. There is only room in the human heart for one object of worship. So, it's God or money. Choose.

"Do we really have to?" "Yes," Jesus says. "We really have to."

Serve, rather than be served. This one's a bit of a tongue twister, but it's even more a perspective twister. Jesus said in Mark 10, "Whoever wants to be great among you will be your servant. Whoever wants to be first among you will be the slave of all, for the Human One didn't come to be served but rather to serve and to give his life to liberate many people" (vv. 43-45). This really goes against our nature, doesn't it? We often seem genetically predisposed to ask this question, whenever we are trying to make a decision: "What's in it for me?" Ultimately, this life is not about what's in it for you, but about loving God and serving others.

"Do we have to?" Jesus says, "Yes, we have to."

Don't Judge. This one may be the toughest of them all in today's culture. We may not like to think of ourselves as judgmental. But when it comes down to it, we do compartmentalize people. We put labels and stickers on them. We separate people out by lifestyle, by class, by race, by sexual orientation, by age, by gender. We build these barriers up, often drawing circles to define who is like us and who is not. And when push comes to shove, like attracts like. But Jesus was pretty clear in Matthew 7. Don't judge, so that you aren't judged. "Why do you see the splinter that's in your brother's or sister's eye, but don't notice the log in your own eye?" (v. 3).

Care for the Hurting. That includes the poor, the imprisoned, the homeless, the sick, the refugee, the skeptic, the grieving. Anyone who feels pushed to the margins of society, lost and forgotten. Jesus said it in Matthew 25: If anyone cares for the least of these, you care for Jesus himself. And yes, that is hard. And even when we do venture out to help those in need, we do it out of a sense of guilt or powerlessness or obligation. How about doing it out of worship?

Out of a sense of connectedness to our fellow human beings? Out of humility? Out of love?

"Do we really have to?" "Yes," Jesus says. "We really do."

Jesus First. Over and over again, Jesus would tell his disciples, the Pharisees, and anyone who would listen that our commitment to God and our citizenship in the Kingdom ranks higher than any other earthly identity, flies higher than any flag, is beyond any border, and even outranks our patriotism to this or any other country.

I know there are pockets of faithful Christians who would conflate the two. God and country. Flag and cross. There's nothing inherently wrong with being patriotic or proud of this country. I most certainly am.

But I think about the exchange between Jesus and Pilate during his trial in John's Gospel. Pilate was trying to squeeze Jesus into nationalistic terms, trying to associate him with one nation's banner, to get him to swear allegiance to one political ideology. But Jesus didn't. He said, in John 18:36, "My kingdom doesn't originate from this world."

Forgive. Turn the other cheek. Walk a second mile. Forgive, as God has forgiven you. Maybe this is the hardest one. It sure feels like it sometimes. It really runs against the grain of our deepest instincts. It's hard enough to love our enemies and pray for our persecutors. But forgiveness is something else entirely. It's certainly a lesson we wish Jesus had never said. Forgiveness is not easy, it takes a long time, and sometimes you think that forgiving someone makes the hurt go away, only to discover the next day it has not, so you have to forgive them again and again and again, like seventy-times-seven times.

"Do we really have to?" "Yes," Jesus said. "We really have to."

Well, there you go. That was by no means an exhaustive list, just the ones that come to mind, maybe because they are the toughest for me. Maybe they are for you. It could be that some of these are harder for you than others. I get that too. But these are all lessons that we have to learn, whether we want to or not.

But here is the important thing to remember: it is not about our works, our efforts, and our abilities to follow Jesus perfectly in every way. Ultimately, it is about two things:

First, it is by God's grace and power alone that we are able to live in this way. It began with the gift of God's image birthed within us from the very beginning, and it continues in the way that God's relentless grace is constantly at work in and through us. It's true: you can't do this on your own. But God can, and does, through Christ.

> ### *It is by God's grace and power alone that we are able to live in this way.*

Second, God's love for you is unwavering. Even when we screw up and don't get it right, we should rest in the assurance that God does not cease caring for us. That love is enough to motivate us to get up, move forward, and try again. Sometimes you'll get it right, and sometimes you won't. But always, God loves you.

And that is indeed good news.

MORAL EXAMPLE THEORY IN SUMMARY

Definition of Sin: We have tarnished and corrupted the image of God that was originally created within us. It has rendered us unable to fully reflect the love of God before others and causes harm to each other and the world.

Definition of Salvation: Through his life, death, and resurrection, Jesus demonstrates for us the way to live and love and empowers us to follow his example.

Pros: It encompasses the whole of Jesus's life and ministry on earth as important for granting us salvation. For those who find the blood imagery of other atonement theories problematic, Moral Example can be useful for advocating for nonviolence.

Cons: It can be perceived as "works-based righteousness," as if it were incumbent on us to do what is necessary.

Response: It empowers us to be a people of self-giving, self-sacrificial love, here and now.

REFLECTING ON THE CROSS

What do you find most difficult about following Jesus?

What difference does it make to see salvation as something for here and now, rather than simply about getting into heaven after you die?

How will you be a more loving, more self-giving person?

CHAPTER 4
RECONCILIATION: JESUS RESTORES YOUR RELATIONSHIP

RECONCILIATION: JESUS RESTORES YOUR RELATIONSHIP

There is a story told about the British landscape painter John Constable, who gained fame for his paintings of beautiful English countrysides in the nineteenth century. He had a son, also named John, who was the oldest of six children, and who kept a diary that chronicled the following story.

John Constable hosted a special exhibition of his latest works, attracting fans of his work from throughout the surrounding area. The largest of the paintings was to be the grand finale and was shrouded by a large curtain that would be removed at the moment of the big reveal.

When that moment came, Constable pulled the cord and parted the curtain. Much to the shock and dismay of the crowd, the painting had been torn. There was a large, gaping tear from top to bottom. The attendees gasped with horror, leaving sad and disappointed.

Later that night, as Constable and his family gathered in their house, his son John walked in, looking scared and remorseful.

"Did you do this?" Constable asked his son.

"Yes," John said, his eyes streaking with tears.

And then, Constable said a remarkable thing, in a tone that was much more merciful and measured than it was angry or punitive.

"How shall we mend it, my dear?"[1]

We learn in Genesis that God created a world filled with beauty, and people in it to be stewards of that beauty and to be in harmonious relationships with each other. But like a giant tear in a masterpiece painting, sin entered the picture, causing a cosmic rift that would alter the course of humanity.

This is the basis of our next explanation of the cross. Jesus came into a world that had been frayed by sin and torn apart by our disobedience, and fulfilled the mission to reconcile the world back to God and human beings with one another.

In a sense, the cross is the answer to the great theological problem posed by sin:

"How shall we mend it?"

RECONCILIATION

If there is anything we learn about God throughout the Bible, it is that God desires to be in relationship with us. There are lots of attributes we know about God, including that God is loving and powerful and holy. But from the very beginning, in the Book of Genesis, God created human beings to be in a relationship with them.

And it works both ways. If we are created in God's image, then we in turn are inherently oriented toward wanting to be in relationship with that same God. We come to conscious realization of that at different points in our lives. Some of us first wondered about God when we were younger, growing up in the church. Some of us longed for God later in life when we wondered about a higher power in the cosmos as we stared up in the sky. And some of us have lived most of our lives as skeptics, only to spark an interest in the possibility of God quite recently.

All those moments point to this singular reality:

God and humans are meant to be in a relationship with each other.

But longing for that relationship and actually living into that relationship are two different things. And sometimes the chasm that we feel between us and God can feel very wide.

It's like the two guys who were on opposite sides of a river. The man on one riverbank called out to the other one, "Hey, how can I get over to the other side?" And the other one says, "*You're* the one on the other side."

You may be feeling every bit of that separation from God in this very moment. You are reading this book right now with some hope that you'll feel close to God like you once did or maybe that you'll feel close to God for the first time. The separation between you and God feels so wide, it's not like you are on opposite sides of a river, you are on opposite sides of a chasm, standing on opposite cliffs, with a wide gorge in between. And the distance is so far that as you look to the other side, God seems so far away and so small you might even question whether God even exists.

It may instead be that your feelings of separation from God are less severe, but real nonetheless. Maybe you're not going through something like a theological or existential crisis, but rather a realization that your relationship with God is not as intimate as it should be. You and God may at least be on "speaking terms"; you just wish you it were easier to listen.

If either of these conditions describes your situation, then the reconciliation understanding of atonement may resonate with you.

This approach to describing the significance of the cross suggests that our wayward behavior and our sinful state have caused a breach, a chasm, a divide in our relationship with God. As a result, we aren't able to hear God clearly, as if static has interfered with our reception of and ability to listen to God's voice. We aren't able to know God's will for us, as if a dizziness in our spirit has ruined our attentiveness to God. And we aren't able to see who we are created to be, as if we are staring at ourselves in a funhouse mirror.

Imagine the worst feeling you have ever felt as a result of a breakup with somebody, and compound it by a thousand. That's what has happened between us and God. The idea of reconciliation helps us understand how Jesus's death on the cross bridges that impossible gap and restores our relationship with God.

RECONCILIATION IN THE BIBLE AND HISTORY

Reconciliation is one of Paul's favorite ways to explain the work of Jesus on the cross. We were separated from God because of our sinful nature and actions. That wide gap could not be removed by our own efforts, so God sent Jesus to bridge that chasm and enable us to be in a full relationship with God once more. And because Jesus reconciled God with humanity, we can then be an agent for reconciliation with each other.

Paul described the reconciling work of Jesus to the Colossians, reminding them (and us) that the source of our separation from God is our sins:

> *Once you were alienated from God and you were enemies with him in your minds, which was shown by your evil actions. But now he has reconciled you by his physical body through death, to present you before God as a people who are holy, faultless, and without blame.*
>
> *(Colossians 1:21-22)*

Paul describes sin in a stark term: evil. And when we see words like that, we often gloss over them with a sense that we are innocent of such egregious sins. But that would be missing Paul's point. Sins of any kind—of any size—are a problem. And more often than not, feelings of separation from God are caused by the smallest and most inconspicuous of sins.

Here's an example of how something so small could be so disruptive.

A few years ago, I decided to give a special gift to my dad for Father's Day. Since his retirement, he had a lot more time to pursue a lifelong interest in fishing. I was eager to replace his older fishing pole with a brand-new one, so I went to one of the local stores, picked out one that I thought was nice, and took it home to my house to get it all ready to give him: new fishing line, new tackle, including a brand-new hook. Everything he would need to just unwrap the pole and use it right away.

I decided to do all this prep work in a comfortable chair in my bedroom. I put the pole together, affixed the reel to the rod, and strung a brand-new fishing line onto the reel. I put some fishing attachments on the end of the line, and then proceeded to put the new hook on the end of it.

Now, I've tied countless hooks to fishing lines in the past. I am no expert fisherman by a long shot, but I have never had an accident putting a hook on a line.

Until that moment.

No, I did not stab myself with the hook. No, I did not cut myself with the line. In some ways, those would have been easier to deal with than what actually happened.

I made a mistake of putting on a hook that was, first of all, really quite small. The eye of the hook—the part where the line goes through—was so small that it was a challenge to get the line to go through it. And then, when it came time to looping and tying the line with a secure knot, the line and the hook flew out of my hand, and the tension built up by having the rod bent toward me caused the end of the line to fly out of my hands, and the hook to sail into the air.

So now, you know what happened. I lost the hook. And again, it was so small that locating it felt next to impossible. I should add at this point that also in my bedroom were a few piles of clean laundry that I was going to fold and put away later. And the carpet, while not a deep shag, was close enough in color as to nearly match the tint of the hook.

And all of this is to say that when the dog came running into the room at that very moment, I leaped to my feet and shooed him out the door.

I picked up my daughters from school and told them not to go in my room. I spent the better part of that evening wearing shoes in my bedroom, with a flashlight, inspecting every nook and cranny of that carpet, inspecting every article of clothing, under every piece of furniture, yet I could not locate that silly little hook.

I slept in the living room that night, because the last thing I wanted was to discover the hook in my bed as I slept.

For an entire weekend, after hours and hours of searching and searching, I could not find that hook.

And I felt separated. Separated from my normal routine, from my preferred life of tranquility, and separated from all that I knew I should be and could be doing.

All because of something so small.

That's the power of sins of any size. You may feel like your life is fine overall and that your situation is a far cry from chaos and trauma. But deep down inside, there are tiny little hooks hiding in the shadow parts of your life, lurking there, ready to wreak havoc if you don't find them and address them. And in that way, you are separated from God, separated from others, and separated from the kind of life God intends for you to live.

Yes, I finally found the hook. But not until I gave up looking. I had surrendered in exasperation. I flopped down in exhaustion on that chair, the same chair where I had tried to hook the line to begin with. I closed my eyes, tilted my head toward the ceiling, and breathed a sigh. Almost as if to say, "You win, stupid hook. Go ahead, stab me now and get it over with. Finish me off once and for all."

And when I opened my eyes, I looked down at the carpet, and there it was. Glistening in the light, as if to taunt me and tease me.

You cannot repair your broken relationship with God on your own. You cannot locate and conquer every little bit of sin in your life by yourself. As we have discovered in every approach to the cross we have studied so far, you cannot earn your salvation. You cannot pay for your sins or set yourself free or earn God's love or repair your separation from God.

It's an idea captured by Augustine, who describes the human condition as a "wide gulf" between us and God, which can be remedied only by Jesus, who bridges that gap:

> But when sin had placed a wide gulf between God and the human race, it was expedient that a Mediator, who alone of the human race was born, lived, and died without sin, should reconcile us to God, and procure even for our bodies a resurrection to eternal life, in order that the pride of man might be exposed and cured through the humility of God.[2]

As with all these atonement theories, reconciliation recognizes that we are helpless to save ourselves. We cannot build a bridge to God; we cannot draw near to God by our own actions.

The only one who can save us is God, and we must surrender ourselves to God's power.

> *We cannot build a bridge to God; we cannot draw near to God by our own actions.*
>
> *The only one who can save us is God, and we must surrender ourselves to God's power.*

RECONCILIATION WITH ONE ANOTHER

The reconciliation understanding of atonement not only describes the repair of our broken relationship with God. It also reminds us of how Christ reconciles us with one another. The Bible is filled with individuals and communities who sought to work through their divisions and were only able to do so through the power and grace of God. Where violence and revenge should prevail, the work of Jesus brings the possibility of forgiveness and healing.

> *Where violence and revenge should prevail, the work of Jesus brings the possibility of forgiveness and healing.*

A prominent example of the call for reconciliation can be found in the Book of Ephesians. The major controversy in the backdrop of Ephesians can be found right in the second chapter. It was Jew vs. Gentile.

Jews understood themselves to be God's chosen people, with whom God had made a covenant. Gentiles were outsiders who did not enjoy this special, close relationship with God. But if they did want to become a part of the Jewish people, Gentiles would have to begin following the laws that made up God's covenant, including the outward and visible sign of circumcision. There was a literal wall in the temple separating Jews from Gentiles, a point beyond which Gentiles were not allowed inside.

On the other hand, from the perspective of many Gentiles, Jews were a unique people with strange laws. Their worship and devotion to only one God made them seem foolish and closed-minded, as did their laws (such as food regulations) that seemed unnecessarily strict.

The early church was made of both Jews and Gentiles, as Paul and other Christian preachers upheld that salvation through Christ had been offered to all, Jew and Gentile alike.

s and attitudes die hard, and you can bet this con-
se cultural division.

even in our society.

longer have the stark discord between Jews and
Gentiles, but you can bet we are still tribalists at heart. Various
divisions exist among people today that are every bit as intense as
the first-century distinction between Jews and Gentiles And Paul
has a razor-sharp insight that disrupts those binary boxes. Basically,
what he says is, "The truth of God, and the heart of God, is bigger
than those boxes."

To the Jews, Paul would say, "Remember." Remember that the
movement of God throughout the Gospels is an ever-widening
circle of God's hospitality to more and more people.

- Where there was a wall that excluded Samaritans, Jesus
  visited the woman at the well.
- Where there was a wall that excluded Canaanites, Jesus
  met a foreigner whose faith impressed him like no other.
- Where there was a wall that excluded children, Jesus told
  the disciples to let them come.
- And when there was a wall that excluded Gentiles, God
  came to Peter in a vision and said there is no more clean
  and unclean.

To the Gentiles, Paul would also say, "Remember." Remember
that grace is not cheap. Paul is very clear to the Gentiles: *Even though
you have not been saved by your good works, you have been saved to
do good works.* The law has not saved you. But the holiness of God
calls you to live a certain way. A way of love, a way of peace, and a
way that transcends division between you and others, between you
and God.

So, if you ask Paul who is right, and pose to him an either/or proposition of which camp is correct, Paul would say this:

> But now, thanks to Christ Jesus, you who once were
> so far away have been brought near by the blood of
> Christ. Christ is our peace. He made both Jews and
> Gentiles into one group. With his body, he broke down
> the barrier of hatred that divided us.
>
> *(Ephesians 2:13-14)*

Why is the church important today? Because we can be the antidote to tribalism, the alternative to the divisiveness that has infected every aspect of our social condition today.

Let's remember, after all, where Paul came from. Before he became the greatest missionary that the world would ever know, he was one of the fiercest opponents of Christianity. And he was a living testimony to the power of God to break down hostility.

Paul was first reconciled with God, and then God was able to reconcile Paul with other people in a remarkable way.

SAUL AND ANANIAS

When we first meet Paul he is known as Saul, and he had gained notoriety throughout the first-century Palestinian world as a persecutor and a murderer of Christians. By his own account in Acts 22, he was responsible for "binding" Christian men and women, throwing them into prison, and even putting them to death. He was an eyewitness to the stoning of Stephen, the first Christian martyr, and served as a part-time bounty hunter, under contract with officials to seek out Christians and bring them to punishment.

That's what he was doing on his way to a city called Damascus, serving out an arrest warrant, doing his job.

He would be the last person you would think God would want to add to the team, the person you would least expect to become the greatest missionary the world would ever know. What could possibly transform his heart? What could possibly transform his hatred?

Make no mistake about it, Paul was a religious terrorist. He committed acts of great violence in the name of religion. But the Book of Acts makes it clear: God had not given up on him. God wanted to transform him. And God was willing to go to any lengths to make it happen.

A blinding light caught Paul and his traveling companions dead in their tracks on the road to Damascus, and Jesus appeared to him and asked, "Why are you persecuting me?" And the light struck Paul blind, to the point where he could not go one step further.

Pretty dramatic stuff. We might even say it was the most dramatic conversion moment in the entire Bible.

And to be sure, this could have been the end of the story of Paul's conversion. That the vision of Jesus and the blinding light was all it took to transform the hatred of his heart into an ambassador of God's love. And the story could have been over right here.

But that's not how transformation works. Do you want to know what does? Do you want to know what God uses to transform the hearts of even the most hateful people into people of love?

Relationships. Relationships with ordinary people like you and me.

Notice that as soon as Paul's eyes went blind, he depended on traveling companions to guide him, step by step, into Damascus. And once he got there, there was a plot twist, in the form of Ananias.

Ananias was a follower of Jesus. He was a prayerful, obedient Christian, who one day was given by God a remarkable mission: to meet Paul face to face. To have a personal encounter with a man whose infamous reputation was as a killer of Christians like himself.

Could you do it? Would you do it? Would you be able to befriend a terrorist? A radicalized fundamentalist? A person who in their very being wanted nothing to do with people like you?

That's what God was saying to Ananias, and again Ananias must have wondered: "God, do you know what you're doing?"

As it turns out, God knew exactly what God was doing. Because no person is out of the reach of God's love. And no amount of hatred in a person's heart too big for God to redeem. Sometimes, it just takes an Ananias.

That Ananias could be you, just like it was for C. P. Ellis and Ann Atwater.

> *No person is out of the reach of God's love.*
> *And no amount of hatred in a person's*
> *heart too big for God to redeem.*

THE BEST OF ENEMIES

Claiborne Paul (C. P.) Ellis was born in Durham, North Carolina in 1927. His family had grown up poor, and Ellis became quite disillusioned with the promise of the American Dream. He worked for several years at a gas station, then got married and had four children. One of his children was both blind and mute. Money was always hard for him to come by, and hardships always seemed to follow him.

His father was a participant in the local Ku Klux Klan, and over time, Ellis determined to fix blame for all of his hardships on the black community. Eventually, Ellis himself joined the Klan, rose in the ranks of leadership, and formed a youth group intent on training young people how to hate. He found in the Klan a sense of empowerment and identity based on hatred of others.

He was Saul.

But God had not given up on him, just as God didn't give up on Saul, just as God doesn't give up on any of us.

So, God called into the picture a woman named Ann Atwater, an African-American civil rights activist living in Durham. It was 1971, when the Durham School Board was faced with growing tension over desegregation. So a community organizer named Bill Riddick put together a series of community meetings called *charrettes*, which were opportunities for people in Durham to come together, listen to each other, speak their truth, and bring to the light the deep injustices and divisions within the heart of their community.

And Bill Riddick asked C. P. Ellis, exalted cyclops of the KKK, and Ann Atwater, civil rights activist, to cochair those meetings.

And God got to work. Over ten days of meetings in the community, the heart of C. P. Ellis was softened. Through the friendship being formed between him and Ms. Atwater, Ellis began to see the hatred of his own heart and how wrong it was to dehumanize people of color. And he even saw how his racism was also holding back white people. He saw that even poor whites could benefit from the civil rights movement. He saw how both blacks and whites faced many of the same economic hardships.

Atwater and Ellis came to know each other as individuals instead of as stereotypes. During these charrette gatherings, Atwater and

Ellis cried together. These meetings often included gospel music. Ellis would clap his hands and stomp his feet, and at one point, Atwater leaned over to him and taught him how to clap because, according to her, "White folks clap an odd beat."

On the last night of the charrette, one thousand people participated, including some of Ellis's fellow Klan members. At the microphone, Ellis held his Klan membership card up and said: "If schools are going to be better by me tearing up this card, I shall do so." Ellis thus renounced the Klan that night and never returned to it. The remaining Klansmen threatened his life and refused to talk to him for the next thirty years. But Ellis and Atwater formed an enduring friendship.

For the rest of his life, Ellis was an avid advocate for civil rights, racial harmony, and economic justice for all. He died in 2005, having made a profound difference in the community.

All because God didn't give up on him, and because Ann Atwater said yes to God.

Their story is captured in the film *The Best of Enemies*. That's a great title, and an even better story. It points to the way that God prefers to work.

The very first words out of Ananias's mouth to Saul were these: "Brother Saul." Not persecutor Saul, or hateful Saul, or simply Saul, but *brother*. Are you able to call others the same, brothers and sisters in the human community?

I wonder if you can be an Ann or an Ananias to someone. Even someone who dehumanizes you and does not wish to have anything to do with you. The story of God's grace is full of plot twists, surprise after surprise. And it could be that God has one for you.

Maybe the same Jesus who reconciled you with God could empower you to be an agent of reconciliation with others.

Would you be open to being used by God in such a surprising way? Would you be open to exploring your own prejudices and narrow views, and allowing God to surprise you, by getting to know someone who is different from you? If the scales from your eyes—and theirs—might fall, we can change the hearts of people like Paul in the world today.

A NEW RELATIONSHIP

There are countless examples of reconciliation between persons where hurt and harm were healed by the grace of God. The story of Koinonia Farm is one such example. Clarence Jordan and others founded Koinonia Farm in Georgia in 1942, emphasizing equality from the outset by paying white and black seasonal workers a fair and equal wage. They also began to build affordable homes to address housing inequality. They remained steadfast in their commitment despite efforts from the KKK and others to force them out. Koinonia Farm still operates as an intentional Christian community today, and its housing ministry eventually blossomed into Habitat for Humanity.

The founders of Koinonia Farm recognized an important truth: Jesus has taken from us the marks of our former allegiances, the marks of sin and disobedience, and freed us to start a brand-new relationship with God, a fresh start on life, and a life of new hope and possibility. Since their founding they have sought to offer the hope of this fresh start, this ministry of reconciliation, to others.

Regardless of what has happened in your past, know that today you can have a fresh, new start. A chance to be in a new relationship with the God who created you, loves you, and reconciled you with God.

SHARING THE SAME SOUL

And then, there is reconciliation that can happen between individuals, in the most poignant and personal way.

In December 2017, *CBS Evening News* ran a story about two preschool girls who refused to live into the binary boxes and the tribalistic tendencies that so many adults tend to live in. Jia Sarnicola is Caucasian, and Zuri Copeland is African-American. They said they are not best friends. They did not even refer to each other as simply "sisters." Instead, they called themselves twins.

Their birthdays are practically on the same day. And they said they were about the same height. And often, they wore matching outfits. The news segment showed footage of them playing on the playground, laughing, smiling, and enjoying each other's companies.

One time, Zuri and Jia were at a birthday party, when an older kid told them that there was no way they could be twins, because they had different skin colors. That remark stung Jia, but she was able to utter this profound retort: "You don't know what you're talking about. We're twins because we share the same soul."

"I was just thrown by just that word," said Valencia, Zuri's mom.[3]

Zuri and Jia understand that which is at the heart of our Christian understanding of humanity: we have all been created in God's image, designed to be in a full relationship with God and with each other. The reconciliation concept of atonement reminds us that sin has broken that relationship, just as systemic sins like racism would divide us from each other.

But in Christ, God comes to repair that relationship, drawing us toward God and toward one another.

And that is our calling as the church, to be God's antidote to tribalism. Even though our default human condition is to categorize people into manageable, ideological and sociological boxes, God calls us to live into the vision of Ephesians, to make

> *an effort to preserve the unity of the Spirit with the peace that ties you together. You are one body and one spirit, just as God also called you in one hope. There is one Lord, one faith, one baptism, and one God and Father of all, who is over all, through all, and in all.*
>
> (Ephesians 4:3-6)

THE CHURCH WE LONG FOR

The reconciling work of Jesus makes possible a vision for the church in which we are not only brought together in unity across our differences, but we can be a unifying voice for a divided world. That kind of church is part of the imagination of God and can be a compelling vision for us to realize today.

Once, at the conclusion of a sermon, I invited people in the pews to call out words and phrases that complete this statement:

"The church I long for is . . ."

The result was one of the most inspired moments in worship that we had had in a long time. People kept calling out words and phrases from all corners of the room, and we couldn't write them down fast enough.

Their responses included these actual words:

Welcoming, unconditionally loving, inclusive, overflowing with love, accepting, committed to Jesus, unified in love, peaceful and warm, always asking questions, always learning, authentic diversity, open to change, trustworthy, does not discriminate, IS going to change the world, works outside its walls, constantly tries to listen, bold and creative, keeps old traditions and finds new ones, is not afraid, sees you, accepts all who Jesus would accept, continues to make God's love real, balances confidence and humility, changes as needed, invests in future generations, has no borders, has no walls, accepting, tolerant, loving, is not satisfied, comfortable in gray areas, okay with saying it doesn't know all the answers, building bridges, united in diversity, willing to struggle.

It was a beautiful moment to share together as a congregation, as the Spirit sparked among us all kinds of qualities of the kind of church God was calling us to be.

How would your church respond to this question? My hope is that the body of Christ, throughout the world, would come to understand what a burdensome privilege it is to be the church. We get to model for a world addicted to tribalism what the grace of God can do when it tears down walls. And we get to decide how we are going to help make that happen.

We have been reconciled to God through Christ. And in Christ, God is reconciling us with each other. The only thing we need to do is surrender to it, and then help make it happen.

RECONCILIATION ATONEMENT IN SUMMARY

Definition of Sin: Sin separates us from God and each other. It tears at the fabric of our relationships and renders us isolated and divided.

Definition of Salvation: Jesus bridges that gap and enables us to live in a full and free relationship with God and other people. The cross tears down the walls and brings us together to be healed, as well as to be healing agents for others.

Pros: It is an easily relatable metaphor for anyone who feels alienated from God or estranged from someone else. It is also relevant to the divisiveness throughout our society.

Cons: To claim that we have a broken relationship with God might suggest that God is distant or absent from us, which undermines our belief in God's imminence and proximity to us in Jesus.

Response: We are called to be reconciling agents of God's love with others, overcoming the tribalism that exists in our culture and healing the world of its polarized divisions.

REFLECTING ON THE CROSS

When has God ever seemed distant or absent from you? What helped you rediscover God's presence in your life?

What evidence of cultural division do you see around you? How might God be calling you to help people reconcile with each other?

What kind of church do you long for?

CHAPTER 5

CLEANSING: JESUS MAKES YOU CLEAN

Psalm 51 • Leviticus 16:11-16

CLEANSING:
JESUS MAKES YOU CLEAN

Dark is the stain that we cannot hide.
What can avail to wash it away?
Look! There is flowing a crimson tide,
brighter than snow you may be today.
"Grace Greater than Our Sin" by Julia Johnson

Around 1846, Ignaz Semmelweis began working at one of the two obstetrical clinics in Vienna. He soon discovered that mothers who delivered children at the First Clinic had a substantially higher mortality rate due to childbed fever than those who delivered at the Second Clinic. The difference was so stark, and so well recognized, that expectant mothers would beg not to be admitted to the First Clinic, even at times choosing to give birth in the street rather than in the clinic.

Semmelweis began studying his own daily routines and the routines of his fellow doctors, trying to understand the difference between the two clinics. Why would the First Clinic have a higher rate of infection, and resulting death, than the Second Clinic? The only major difference he could find was that the First Clinic trained doctors, while the Second Clinic trained midwives. Eventually he realized that the medical students at the First Clinic, who also performed autopsies, were transmitting material from corpses to the mothers in the delivery room. The midwives in training at the Second Clinic, who did not work with corpses, were not contaminating their patients this way. Semmelweis proposed that doctors should wash their hands with a chlorine solution. When they did this, as you might imagine, the rate of childbed fever fell dramatically at the First Clinic, quickly matching the rate at the Second Clinic.

Dr. Semmelweis connected childbed fever with the failure of doctors to perform the simple but critical act of washing their hands. From that point on, he not only washed his own hands, he insisted that other people wash theirs, for the sake of protecting themselves and others. It made a huge difference.

But despite his insistence that other doctors do something as simple as hand washing, many would not believe him. Even so, he continued to insist on the importance of hand-washing as a simple yet effective way to save lives.[1]

CLEANSING FROM SIN

This story is a compelling metaphor for an understanding of the death of Jesus sometimes called "expiation," which is a fancy word for *cleansing*. It is based on the idea that sin is a stain from which we need God to cleanse us.

The Bible contains numerous passages depicting sin in this way, as a filthy, dirty blemish that must be removed with the proper cleaning agents.

One of those Scriptures is Psalm 51, which contains David's powerful confession after his sins of adultery and murder were brought to light. "Wash me and I will be whiter than snow.... Create a clean heart for me, God," David says (vv. 7, 10).

The shock of David's actions is not just that it involved adultery and murder. It's horrible, but not all that surprising. Other people committed those sins in the Bible. The shock is that this was *King David* who committed them. He is hands down the most highly regarded king in the whole Old Testament. His predecessor Saul never had an affair (that we know of), despite getting it wrong in plenty of his own ways. His successor Solomon never committed a murder so heinous, even though he messed up plenty as well. But the great King David, the one who is glorified above them all, committed some of the most harmful and violent sins in the whole Bible.

The biblical writers could have chosen not to include this story. That they kept not only the story, but described God's response to it via Nathan the prophet, is the Bible's way of saying that none of us—not even the most pious appearing among us—is impervious to the stain of sin.

When I was a youth, I heard a preacher say that there are four conditions in which we find ourselves most susceptible to temptation. They can be remembered with the acronym "HALT." H-A-L-T. We are most likely to sin when we are hungry, angry, lonely, and tired. I've remembered that ever since, and when I find myself in any of those four situations, I know that that I have to be on guard, because the temptation to compromise my convictions is greater than usual.

But what's interesting is that this tragic story of David would add a fifth word to that acronym, *successful*, and make it "HALTS." For it is when David was successful that he was most tempted to sin.

At the start of 2 Samuel 11, David and the Israelites had recently won a victory against the armies of the Arameans and the Ammonites. And we get the sense that David had reached a point where there was just no challenge anymore for him in conquering other people. When springtime rolled around, he didn't even bother leading the army to battle. He was so confident in their victory that he stayed home to rest on his laurels and enjoy the spoils of his victory, while his general Joab led the army instead.

The biblical principle here is that just because things might be going well in your life, it does not mean you can let your guard down in your daily battle against sin. In fact, you may be the kind of person that is most vulnerable when you are feeling most confident. That was David's problem.

He had become so used to conquering and controlling that when he saw Bathsheba, he saw her as another acquisition, and then saw her husband as another obstacle in his way, another problem to be eliminated. Sin blinds us into thinking that we can handle power and control. Remember what the serpent told Adam and Eve? Eat the fruit, and you will be like God. That's the temptation.

In the very next chapter, the prophet Nathan comes to David with the powerful pronouncement and indictment by way of a parable. Nathan describes for David a rich man with many flocks, who took and slaughtered a poor man's beloved lamb to feed a guest rather than kill one of his own. David pronounces harsh judgment against such a cruel act, to which Nathan responds: "You are that man." David had the whole kingdom at his disposal, yet he took the wife of another man, one of his own loyal soldiers. Confronted with this reality, David acknowledges his sin.

And so we have Psalm 51. David's confession.

In a way, we are kind of left to wonder if we would even have Psalm 51 in our Bible if Nathan hadn't shown up. Would David have confessed if his sins were never brought to light?

We might wonder that about David, but we do not have to wonder that about ourselves. This psalm invites you to a preemptive confessional: to confess the stain of your sins, even before your sins come to light.

Psalm 51 contains a template for such a confession based on the cleansing work of God:

> *Wash me thoroughly from my iniquity,*
> *and cleanse me from my sin....*
>
> *Purge me with hyssop, and I shall be clean;*
> *wash me, and I shall be whiter than snow....*
>
> *Create in me a clean heart, O God,*
> *and put a new and right spirit within me.*
> *(vv. 2, 7, 10 NRSV)*

Whenever you see the word *heart* in the Bible, remember that the ancient Israelites understood the heart as the seat of intelligence and emotion, the core of one's being. David did not just ask for a change in his feelings, but a complete reboot of his values, his perspective, and his behavior.

David said, "[God,] you desire truth in the inward being; . . . teach me wisdom in my secret heart" (v. 6 NRSV). When David confessed his sins, God graciously forgave him and helped him to make things right.

And so it is with Jesus, whose work on the cross is the "hyssop" that not only cleanses us of our sins. It creates a brand-new heart, and orients us within a whole new life.

THE SCAPEGOAT

This cleansing work of Jesus is based on a New Testament understanding that he is the fulfillment of the Hebrew sacrificial system and the scapegoat that took upon himself the sins of the people.

We remember that several of the laws in the Old Testament concerned the physical act of cleansing, calling for the Israelites to scrub up, wash up, and clean up.

Consider Leviticus 16, which describes the ritual for the Day of Atonement or Day of Reconciliation. It is, in many ways, a cleansing ritual. Instead of soapy water and hand sanitizer, there is the blood of a bull and a goat. Instead of a washbasin or bathroom sink, there is an incense pan. Yet the goal is the cleansing of sin that has accumulated throughout the year. The high priest Aaron is the key figure in the story, and he follows the precise formula given by God to go through the cleansing of the people's sins. The ritual must be performed once a year in the Tabernacle (and later, the temple), and it was designed to purge all the sins from the sanctuary—even those the people had committed unintentionally.

Much of the terminology may seem odd, and the images feel antiquated. But there is one more important dimension to this story. It occurs just six chapters prior, in Leviticus 10. Because here we also find the high priest Aaron under a very different set of circumstances. It turns out that Aaron had four sons. And two of them had done something to break the commandments of God. The details of their offense are not fully given, as the whole episode is described in only two verses in Leviticus 10. But what is clear is that because of their transgressions, God was not pleased, and these two sons of Aaron died.

We then get a full sense of what is really happening in Leviticus 16. Once we get past the bizarre imagery, and the peculiar business of taking burning coals on an incense pan and sprinkling incense to perfume the offering, and once we get past the slaughtering of the goat and the sprinkling of its blood, and if we remember that this is a ritual of cleansing that comes as a gift from God, then we come to see what is really happening here:

We see a man, overcome with grief, not just performing ritualistic cleansing for the guilt of a nation, but trying to cleanse his own guilt, and the guilt of his past. And it is here that humanity discovers that some stains are too hard to just scrub away with soap and water. The deeper stains of guilt and shame require something stronger, something far beyond our ability to cleanse on our own.

Right now, you may have stains that you cannot get out. Like Aaron, there are haunting regrets that have filled your past. And these regrets are easily identified by the way they each begin with the same two words:

If only.

If only I had been more disciplined, I would not have given in to that temptation.

If only I had handled that situation differently, I would not have made such a dumb mistake.

If only I were a better parent or a better spouse or a better communicator.

If only I had a different past or had a different environment growing up or knew then what I know now about myself.

If only, if only, if only.

As we have come to discover along the way in this journey, there are a lot of ways to define sin. Some of them are based on what we have done. Some are based on what we haven't done. Some are based solely on the condition into which we are born, and the ways that culture and environment have conditioned us to live.

And then there is a way to look at sin that covers them all: that sin is a stain that we cannot get out on our own. A stain of guilt, a stain of shame. The stain of sin.

And so it is that the old high priest Aaron went in to the Holy of Holies to make a burnt offering to the Lord and cast the sins of the people on the sacrificial animal.

The Day of Atonement ritual called for two goats: one to be killed and sacrificed on the altar, and the other to receive the sins of the people and be cast out into the wilderness. That was called the scapegoat, the one on whom the guilt, the sins of the people were placed. That was the thing that became dirty, so that the people of God could become clean.

By the time the New Testament writers began reflecting on what the cross of Jesus meant, this idea of the scapegoat became an influential part of their understanding. They identified Jesus as the new scapegoat, the agent of cleansing, the one who would become dirty with our sins so that we might be cleansed of all our sins, our shame, and our guilt.

Look at how the author of Hebrews describes Jesus as the new Aaron, our new high priest, and the scapegoat that makes us clean from our sins:

> But Christ has appeared as the high priest of the good
> things that have happened. He passed through the
> greater and more perfect meeting tent, which isn't made
> by human hands (that is, it's not a part of this world).
> He entered the holy of holies once for all by his own

blood, not by the blood of goats or calves, securing our deliverance for all time. If the blood of goats and bulls and the sprinkled ashes of cows made spiritually contaminated people holy and clean, how much more will the blood of Jesus wash our consciences clean from dead works in order to serve the living God? He offered himself to God through the eternal Spirit as a sacrifice without any flaw. (9:11-14)

Other passages include Titus 3:5:

He saved us because of his mercy, not because of righteous things we had done. He did it through the washing of new birth and the renewing by the Holy Spirit.

And in the first epistle of John, we hear the it most succinctly:

But if we live in the light in the same way as he is in the light, we have fellowship with each other, and the blood of Jesus, his Son, cleanses us from every sin. (1:7)

THE CLEANSING IDEA THROUGHOUT HISTORY

The understanding of the cross based on cleansing has been influential throughout history, in some of our greatest thinkers and hymn writers.

Tertullian described sin as a state of being "unclean": "Every Soul, then, by reason of its birth, has its nature in Adam until it is born again in Christ; moreover, it is unclean all the while that it remains without this regeneration...and because unclean, it is actively sinful."[2]

In his commentary on the Epistle to the Romans, Origen wrote,

> Although the holy Apostle teaches many wonderful things about our Lord Jesus Christ which are said mysteriously about him, in this passage he has given special prominence to something which, I think, is not readily found in other parts of Scripture.... God put him forward *as an expiation by his blood, to be received by faith*. This means that by the sacrifice of Christ's body God has made expiation on behalf of men and by this has shown his righteousness, in that he forgave their previous sins, which they had committed in the service of the worst possible tyrants.[3]

In his work "On Perfection," Gregory of Nyssa wrote: "Christ, being an *expiation by his blood*, teaches each one thinking of this to become himself a propitiation, sanctifying his soul by the mortification of his members."[4]

It is something that Flannery O'Connor came to recognize in her own life. She is widely considered to be one of the greatest Southern spiritual writers of the twentieth century, and in her published private journal, she acknowledged the way that the sin within her served as a kind of foreign body that eclipsed the glory of God in her life:

> Dear God, I cannot love Thee the way I want to. You are the slim crescent of a moon that I see and my self is the earth's shadow that keeps me from seeing all the moon. The crescent is very beautiful and perhaps that is all one like I am should or could see; but what I am afraid of, dear God, is that my self shadow will grow so large that it blocks the whole moon, and that I will

Atonement - attain forgiveness for sin
Expiation - clear away the record

judge myself by the shadow that is nothing. I do not know you God because I am in the way. Please help me to push myself aside....

Oh God please make my mind clear.

And then, she ends with these words:

Please make it clean.[5]

The cleansing idea of atonement would become the basis of a stanza from the great hymn "Rock of Ages":

Nothing in my hand I bring,
simply to the cross I cling;
naked, come to thee for dress;
helpless, look to thee for grace;
foul, I to the fountain fly;
wash me, Savior, or I die.

PROS AND CONS OF CLEANSING ATONEMENT THEORY

Now, there may be some of us who are troubled by this understanding of Jesus's death on the cross, for again, every approach has its pros and cons, and we do not all have to agree. There are those who are troubled by the image of a God who demands the taking of a life for the saving of humanity. For some, the whole scapegoat imagery of Jesus is a tough jump to make in the context of modern times.

But here is something we all can agree on: We all know what it's like to have stains in our lives that we cannot remove. We are haunted by memories of our past, just like Aaron was haunted by the skeletons in his own family's closet.

Like a wine stain on a carpet, or a paint stain on clothing, the guilt and shame from our past just lingers on our souls and it is impossible to scrub it away, even as hard as we try.

Gripping addictions. Bad choices. Private secrets. Failed short-cuts and quick fixes. And try as you might to clean up your life, maybe you're tired of scrubbing. And try as you might, there's always residue that remains.

Discontent with life. Anxiety about the future. Strains in your relationships. Painful memories. Haunting guilt.

The Bible says that we do not need to clean our own life. We need only depend on what God has offered to us through Jesus Christ. Because on the cross and through the empty tomb, God's very own heart has been poured out for all creation. To cleanse and purify even the nastiest stains.

> *We do not need to clean our own life.*
> *We need only depend on what God has*
> *offered to us through Jesus Christ.*

All of us are in need of that which washes us and makes us whiter than snow. This concept of atonement claims that through the cross, as we confess our sins, we receive the all-purpose, all-powerful, stain-fighting work of Jesus Christ.

And we can be made clean.

Many of you, I'm sure, have heard of Murphy's Law. Some of you may even swear that you are currently living by Murphy's Law. Some of you may have written the book on Murphy's Law. Put simply, it says that "Anything that can go wrong will go wrong."

But you may not be as familiar with another such law, this one is called Imbesi's Law of the Conservation of Filth: It says, "In order for something to become clean, something else must become dirty."

If you think about it, it's true. Whether you are taking a shower, scrubbing dishes, or washing a car, you'll notice that dirt doesn't just ("poof") disappear. It has to go somewhere. For dishes, body parts, and automobiles to get clean, dishwater, washcloths, and sponges need to get dirty.

Imbesi's Law is a practical law. But it's also a biblical and theological law too. In order for sin to go away, sin has to go somewhere. For us to become clean, to have our sin removed, something—or someone—has to become dirty.

And from the Bible's perspective, that "thing" that became dirty so that we might be clean is the blood of Jesus Christ. There is only one true, effective way to fully remove the blot of sin from a person's life. It is through the spotless, perfect blood of Jesus Christ. It is that blood that took our sin, to clean us and free us.

First John 1:8-9 says, "If we say that we have no sin, we deceive ourselves, and the truth is not in us. If we confess our sins, he who is faithful and just will forgive us our sins and cleanse us from all unrighteousness" (NRSV).

All we have to do is confess our sins and allow Jesus Christ to cleanse us of those things.

What this means, of course, is that we do not have to clean ourselves. And it's a good thing. Because the more we try to clean up ourselves, to cleanse ourselves from our own sins, the more we are likely to make things even worse. Sometime after Imbesi's Law came out, someone named Freeman added an extension. So now Imbesi's Law with Freeman's extension reads: "In order for something to become clean, something else must become dirty. But you can get everything dirty without getting anything clean."

It's a whole lot easier to spread dirt around than it is to clean dirt up. And it's a whole lot easier for human beings, in the effort to rid themselves of their own sins, to infect other people with those sins. There is only one way to fully be cleansed of sin—that is through Jesus Christ.

TWO BOWLS

But there is another way to think about cleansing, especially in the context of the Gospel accounts of Jesus's death. The Gospels paint a contrasting view of two people and two bowls of water and two different ways to wash.

First, consider Pontius Pilate, who followed his sentencing of Jesus to death by washing his hands. Perhaps he had grown weary of the debate and the competing voices between his own conscience and the Jerusalem crowds. Perhaps he had sensed Jesus's innocence but cowered in fear of the growing mob. Perhaps we would want to give Pilate some credit for at least considering the correct choice during his deliberation. But when he washed his hands, he absolved himself of any opportunity to do what was costly, what was risky, and what was right.

In his book *The Cross and the Cellar : Meditations on the Last Seven Words of Christ*, Anglican priest Morton Kelsey describes the moral choice that Pilate had to make:

> Pilate receives most of the blame for Jesus' death, and yet Pilate didn't want to crucify the man. Why did Pilate condemn Jesus? Because Pilate was a coward. He cared more about his comfortable position than

he did about justice. He didn't have the courage to stand for what he knew was right. It was because of this relatively small flaw in Pilate's character that Jesus died on a cross. Whenever you and I are willing to sacrifice someone else for our own benefit, whenever we don't have the courage to stand up for what we see is right, we step into the same course that Pilate took.[6]

That is a biting accusation against Pilate. And if it makes us squirm, it is because we can see our own propensity to be as guilty as Pilate. We would be remiss if we relegated Pilate to a distance, thinking that because he was a person of power, prestige, and authority, he is far removed from our ability to do anything nearly as vile as he did. But the truth is, we are not much different.

His decision was antithetical to the meaning of the cross, which calls us to take the narrow, more complicated path. Whereas the Pilates of this world will choose what is easy and expedient, followers of Jesus are called to live a cruciform life, a life of service and self-surrender. In contrast to the way of violence and appeasement, disciples are called to peace, self-sacrifice, and love.

Ultimately, the hand-washing bowl of Pilate is a direct contrast to the foot-washing bowl of Jesus. On the night before he died, just hours before Pilate washed his hands, Jesus assumed the role of a servant and washed the disciples' feet. And then, he gave them a new commandment: "Love one another. Just as I have loved you, you also should love one another. By this everyone will know that you are my disciples, if you have love for one another" (John 13:34-35).

Ponder this question: Are you a foot washer or a hand washer? Will you offer yourself in self-giving love to others, or will you choose the less complicated way of self-centeredness? Will you follow a road that is marked by cowardice or a road that leads to a cross? Will you choose a love for power or the path of powerless love?

> *Are you a foot washer or a hand washer?*
> *Will you offer yourself in self-giving*
> *love to others, or will you choose the less*
> *complicated way of self-centeredness?*

All of us, without exception, contain the filthy contaminants of a sinful life. God has been at work in us, performing a kind of autopsy on our souls, identifying that within us which is eclipsing the glory of God and preventing us from fully loving God and others.

What does your autopsy report say today? Lingering bad habits? Unhealthy choices? Private secrets? Shortcuts and quick fixes? Greed and avarice? Boastful pride?

Whatever your diagnosis is, your symptoms are clear: Discontent with life. Anxiety about the future. Strains in your relationships. Painful memories. Haunting guilt.

And the words from Dr. Semmelweis ring in our ears: "For God's sake, wash your hands."

Let's remember that we cannot clean up our own life. Instead, we need only depend on what God has offered to us through Jesus Christ. Because on the cross and through the empty tomb, God's very own heart has been poured out for all creation. To cleanse and purify even the nastiest stains.

The cross cleanses, purifies, and washes us of our sins. And if we confess our sins, we receive the all-purpose, all-powerful, stain-fighting work of Jesus Christ.

THE CLEANSING ATONEMENT THEORY IN SUMMARY

Definition of Sin: Sin is a stain that we cannot cleanse on our own. It is more than just a superficial account of our wrongdoings. Sin sinks deep into our innermost being, affecting the way we think, act, feel, and relate to others.

Definition of Salvation: Jesus is the fulfillment of Hebrew understanding of the scapegoat. He cleanses us of our sins by taking sin upon himself. He "becomes dirty" so that we might be "made clean."

Pros: This idea of Christ's death acknowledges how powerless we are to remove sin on our own. It is also deeply rooted in Old Testament imagery and scriptural support throughout the Bible.

Cons: Some may be troubled by the antiquated paradigms of the Hebrew sacrificial system.

Response: Will we follow the example of Jesus or Pilate? Will we be washed in the basin of service to others or wash ourselves of the responsibility to act in love?

REFLECTING ON THE CROSS

When was there a time when you had a stain that you could not remove on your own? What did you ultimately do about it?

What would it look like for you to surrender to the cleansing power of Jesus? What difference will that make in you?

How will you follow in the example of Jesus and not Pilate? How will you choose the way of self-sacrifice instead of the way of self-preservation?

CHAPTER 6

CHRISTUS VICTOR: JESUS GIVES YOU THE VICTORY

CHAPTER 6

Colossians 2:6-15 • Matthew 28:1-20

CHRISTUS VICTOR: JESUS GIVES YOU THE VICTORY

By now you have likely noted that the common thread among all these approaches to understanding Christ's death and its meaning—and how it brings us salvation—is that we cannot save ourselves. Regardless of how each metaphor defines sin, we are helpless to overcome it on our own. We cannot break free from it, we cannot pay its penalty, we cannot restore our relationship with God, we are unable to display the fullness of God's image in us, and we cannot cleanse ourselves from its stains.

Our inability to save ourselves is most pronounced in this final image to understand Jesus's work. We cannot defeat sin on our own. But in Jesus, we can be victorious.

The idea of Christus Victor, or "Christ the Victor," is joyous and celebrative. It immediately conjures up the feelings of triumphant euphoria that are embedded in our competitive and sporting culture. The old ABC's *Wide World of Sports* television program began with the iconic words, "The thrill of victory...and the agony of defeat." Christus Victor is built on that same dichotomy: even though sin defeats us and fills us with agony, Jesus raises us up in victory and enables us to feel the thrill of new life.

So, the place to begin in understanding and appreciating this image for yourself is to think about how you might feel defeated by sin in your life.

The ancient Greek story of Sisyphus can be seen as a metaphor for the overwhelming power of sin to defeat us.

Sisyphus was a mortal characterized by trickery and a disdain for the gods. His deceitfulness enabled him to cheat death on more than one occasion, and as a result, he fell out of favor with Zeus, king of the gods. As punishment, Zeus condemned Sisyphus to eternity in the Underworld, with one and only one task to accomplish: push a gigantic rock up and over a hill.

The first time Sisyphus tried to push the rock up the hill, he started at the base of the mountain, trying with all his might to move it up the steep slope. He succeeded at getting it near the top, almost over the hill, but he was fatigued and the weight of the rock and the pull of gravity caused the rock to tumble back to the base of the hill.

Over and over again, Sisyphus has tried to push the rock over the hill. And to this day, he is still trying. With endless perseverance, he begins at the base of the mountain. He succeeds every time in getting the rock near the top. But every time he comes just a foot close enough, he fatigues, he slips, or he goes over a rough spot, and the rock comes tumbling back down.

Now, remember, this is not a true story. It is a mythological tale. But it does communicate some resonant truth in the human experience. All of us are like Sisyphus. We wake up every morning at the base of the day's mountain, knowing full well of all the gigantic boulders that we will be pushing and lifting before day's end.

Perhaps no other story in ancient Greek mythology communicates our Christian understanding of sin and the utter defeatism that it leaves in its wake. Each day, encumbered by enormous physical, mental, and emotional exhaustion, we attempt to live the kind of life we believe we are created to live. We push with all our might, trying to overcome our sinful habits, the shame and guilt from our past, and the temptations that weigh us down.

And like Sisyphus, the moment we get close is the moment things fall apart. Gravity becomes greater than our strength. Our rock tumbles down to earth. And we are left to end each day wondering to ourselves, "If only there was a way to overcome that giant boulder."

Well, there is.

WHO WILL ROLL AWAY THE STONE?

Just ask the women in Mark's Gospel who showed up early on the first day of the week. They had come to the tomb in which Jesus was laid after his death with spices to anoint the body, and they were beset with grief. This Jesus, who had touched all their lives, was now dead and buried. They had heard the eyewitness accounts. They knew the events of the trial. They had not stopped crying since the earthquake and the darkness. This Jesus, who was their friend, their teacher, their spiritual leader, was gone.

Their anguish was symbolized in a stone.

A large stone had been placed at the entrance to Jesus's tomb. In Mark 16:3, the women coming to anoint his body asked themselves the question: "Who's going to roll the stone away from the entrance for us?"

This powerful question was asked literally and metaphorically. In order for them to get to the body, to pay their respects, to touch for the last time the remains of their dear friend, they had to find a way to roll away the giant boulder standing in the way.

But on a much deeper level, they were struggling with what to do with the crushing weight of grief and despair that had taken over their hearts. The reality of death had set into their hearts and formed a sense of utter defeat within their lives. What were they going to do?

Before we get to what happens next, let's stay here for a minute. Think about how you would answer this question: What are the stones that are blocking your pathway to a free and full life? What gigantic boulders do you get up every morning to push? What is causing you a feeling of utter defeat? Your list may be long, and chief among them may be the reality of your own mortality.

> *What are the stones that are blocking*
>
> *your pathway to a free and full life?*
>
> *What gigantic boulders do you get*
>
> *up every morning to push?*

Luke tells us what happened next:

> *Very early in the morning on the first day of the week, the women went to the tomb, bringing the fragrant spices they had prepared. They found the stone rolled away from the tomb, but when they went in, they didn't find the body of the Lord Jesus. They didn't know what*

> *to make of this. Suddenly, two men were standing*
> *beside them in gleaming bright clothing. The women*
> *were frightened and bowed their faces toward the*
> *ground, but the men said to them, "Why do you look for*
> *the living among the dead? He isn't here, but has been*
> *raised. Remember what he told you while he was still in*
> *Galilee, that the Human One must be handed over to*
> *sinners, be crucified, and on the third day rise again."*
>
> (Luke 24:1-7)

Whatever gigantic obstacles you face from day to day, remember this, with certainty in your spirit and clarity in your voice, with hope in your eyes and power in your witness: God rolled away the stone for the women.

And God has rolled away your stone as well! Not just the stone that blocked the entrance to the cave, but the stone that blocks the freedom of human hearts. A stone that humans could not budge with their own efforts and their own accord. God had done it for the women long ago, and God does it for us.

With more strength than Sisyphus could muster, God took the weight of the world's rock, pushed it up that hill, picked it up, and drop-kicked it into eternity. God can roll away stones!

It is what inspired Paul to write to the Corinthian church, "'Where, O death, is your victory? Where, O death, is your sting?' The sting of death is sin, and the power of sin is the law. But thanks be to God, who gives us the victory through our Lord Jesus Christ" (1 Corinthians 15:55-57 NRSV).

There is no greater stone that we face, no greater force that defeats us as human beings, than the cold, hard reality of death. Every other thing we face pales in comparison to that reality. But Paul says in no uncertain terms that God has defeated death. Removed its sting. Rendered it impotent. Powerless against humans.

Paul's words inspired Charles Wesley to write one of the greatest Easter hymns of the Christian faith, "Christ the Lord Is Risen Today." Two stanzas in particular capture the glorious triumph of Jesus over the grave, and the victory we can now have over sin:

> Lives again our glorious King, Alleluia!
> Where, O death, is now thy sting? Alleluia!
> Once he died our souls to save, Alleluia!
> Where's thy victory, boasting grave? Alleluia!
>
> Soar we now where Christ has led, Alleluia!
> Following our exalted Head, Alleluia!
> Made like him, like him we rise, Alleluia!
> Ours the cross, the grave, the skies, Alleluia!

The "Alleluia" of Easter became the basis for the Christus Victor image of Christ's death and resurrection, espoused by such notable church thinkers as Origen, Gregory of Nyssa, and Augustine.

Ambrose, the fourth-century Bishop of Milan, described Christ's victory using the metaphor of chains that Jesus broke, liberating humanity from the bonds of sin:

> Jesus approached the snares, to set Adam free: he
> came to liberate what had perished. We were all held
> in the toils; no one could rescue another, for no one
> could deliver himself.... Rather he broke the bonds
> and loosed them, and looking out through the snares,
> and rising up above the toils, he called to himself the
> Church, so that the Church also might learn how to
> escape being held by the bonds.[1]

The story of the Resurrection is a story of victory. It is a story of how we are victorious, not through our own actions, but through what God has done. It is a story of what God has done that we cannot do ourselves.

God has rolled away the stone. God has raised Jesus from the dead. God has removed the sting of death and granted for us ultimate triumph over its power. God is victorious over death, and so are we.

And if God can defeat death for us, God can defeat everything else that weighs us down.

All we have to do, by the power of the Holy Spirit, is receive that victory for ourselves and, more importantly, act victorious.

LIVING VICTORIOUSLY

Theologian Alister McGrath recounts a story of an American soldier held captive in a Japanese prisoner-of-war camp in World War II. As the days went by, he and his fellow soldiers waited in isolation, wondering about the condition of the other service people, speculating on how the war was going, and worrying about whether they would live to see the next day.

One day, they overheard their captors as they listened to a short-wave radio deliver the news: the Allied forces had won. The war was over. Freedom for them and all the other prisoners was now a possibility. They could hardly believe what they were hearing. The joy of the news slowly began to settle in.

Still, as they looked around at the conditions in their cell and throughout the camp around them, everything still appeared the same. They were still in captivity, and their captors were still in charge. It would still be weeks before Allied forces would arrive to set them free. So, in the meantime, nothing really had changed.

Except for this: victory had already been secured. And for them, that made all the difference in the world. Even though they were still technically imprisoned, their outlook completely changed. They began to rejoice and see themselves as free people. With their spirits renewed and their hopes held high, they smiled, laughed, sang songs, and began to live into the freedom that they knew had already been guaranteed for them.[2]

This is the essence of Christus Victor, and this is the power of the Resurrection. Not only did Jesus achieve victory over sin and death, he guarantees victory for you, over everything that has kept you defeated.

> *Not only did Jesus achieve victory*
> *over sin and death, he guarantees*
> *victory for you, over everything*
> *that has kept you defeated.*

The only real question that remains is this: Will you receive the power of that victory and begin to live into the freedom that Jesus has won for you?

Now that you are free in Christ, will you act free in Christ?

ONE MORE SURPRISE

In Matthew's Easter Gospel, he takes the Easter story one step further. One step beyond any of the other Gospels, for one more surprise.

After the women received the good news from the angel, and as they were walking away in fear, trying to figure out whether this was really good news or not, Jesus popped out of nowhere. As if the sight of the boulder's removal and the news at the empty tomb weren't shocking enough, now Jesus surprised them. To greet them. To encourage them. To remind them that he was always with them.

Because Matthew wants to remind us that no matter what we are dealing with, whether we are in a high or a low or a plateau, Jesus is with us as we are traveling through life, never to leave us. That's why Matthew ends his Gospel the way no other Gospel does. With Jesus saying to his disciples, "Look, I myself will be with you every day until the end of this present age" (Matthew 28:20).

Matthew's Easter message is clear. No matter what you are facing, and no matter how much sin is weighing you down, Jesus journeys with you, right by your side, and gives you victory over all that weighs you down.

And the moment we realize that, it changes everything. As Hebrews says, because of what Jesus has done on the cross and what God has done in the Resurrection, God has set us free from our captivity and fear.

In other words, God has given us the victory, and nothing is ever the same. The way we live, and the way we face death. The way we face hardship and fight temptation. Even the way we live when all seems to be going well is different, because it is in Jesus and his resurrection that we have victory. In the words of Eugene Bartlett's famous hymn "Victory in Jesus":

> Oh victory in Jesus, my Savior forever!...
> He plunged me to victory beneath the cleansing flood.[3]

APPLYING CHRISTUS VICTOR: CONQUERING VIOLENCE

Perhaps the most significant application of the Christus Victor image is in the way it provides a nonviolent understanding of the cross. Many see it as defeating the need for violence itself as a means for redemption.

Theologians such as Walter Wink, one of the most significant thinkers in the area of nonviolence, have come to understand our culture's addiction to violence as itself evidence of the pervasive nature of sin. Jesus's death on the cross came as a result of his subversion of the worldly view that justice can only be achieved through the exacting of violence as punishment.

Wink writes:

> Through the history of his people's violent and nonviolent struggle for survival, Jesus discovered a way of opposing evil without becoming evil in the process. Here at last was a full-blown alternative to the politics of "redemptive" violence.[4]

Christ's triumph over the need for violence is reiterated in *Saved from Sacrifice: A Theology of the Cross*, in which author S. Mark Heim sees the cross as not only saving us from our sins, but from the need for blood atonement:

> Scapegoating sacrifice is the stumbling block we placed between God and us. It is a root sin buried in our life together. The passion is a divine act revealing, reversing, and replacing our redemptive violence, which we so long and tenaciously hid from ourselves in the name of the sacred.... God saved us from our

form of reconciliation, healed us of our dependence
on that sad medicine.[5]

Christus Victor may resonate with you on many levels. It offers
the promise of victory over the sins that have weighed you down, and
the burdens that you carry as a result. And it provides an alternative
to the violent imagery of the other atonement theories, which you
might deem to be too antiquated to be relevant to your faith. You
ultimately may claim the words of the hymn, "Lift High the Cross":

> Lift high the cross, the love of Christ proclaim
> till all the world adore his sacred name.
>
> So shall our song of triumph ever be:
> Praise to the Crucified for victory!

JESUS CHRIST: OUR SAVIOR

Throughout this text, we have explored some of the most
prevalent and popular understandings of the cross from biblical,
historical, and contemporary perspectives. Again, there is no
agreement throughout the church as to which theory is best, nor
should there be. We are not only allowed to but also encouraged to
come to our own prayerful discernment regarding how Jesus's work
on the cross is most meaningful to us. Whatever our conclusions,
we are drawn into a larger, richer heritage of Christians who have
interpreted their salvation in much the same way.

Ultimately, it is incumbent on us to not only have clarity about
what the cross means, but we should also discover what the cross
calls us to do.

The image of substitution calls us to thanksgiving and praise of
Jesus, who did for us what we could not do for ourselves.

Ransom imagery calls us to a life worthy of the freedom Jesus secured for us.

The idea of moral influence calls us to fully reflect the image of God that is within us, in the way we share God's love with others.

Reconciliation calls us to repair broken relationships and bring healing to the divisions that separate us from one another.

The image of cleansing calls us to repentance, confessing our sins and seeking the power of Jesus to wash us and make us clean.

Christus Victor calls us to live triumphantly over sin, and overcome the systemic sins that oppress others.

No matter what image (or images) you ultimately claim for yourself, we should remember that old adage: we are not saved by our works, but we are saved to do good works.

That is the power of Christ's atonement.

A FINAL IMAGE

One early Saturday morning, I was sitting on a beach chair overlooking Pass-a-Grille Beach in St. Petersburg, one of my favorite spots in the area. I had a cup of coffee, a laptop computer, and a prayer that God would give me some kind of inspiration for my Easter morning message.

And that inspiration came just a few minutes after I sat down.

Into my view came a woman slowly pacing along the shoreline, with a metal detector in her hand. You've seen people like this. Scanning back and forth, searching for whatever lost treasures are buried in the sand. Every few steps, she would reach down with her strainer basket, scoop up a big hunk of sand and sift through it, discovering nothing, and continue her walk.

When she was directly in my line of sight, she stop[...] did something extraordinary. She took off what appeared [...] wedding ring, closed her eyes, and tossed it in the sand, hard enough to bury it out of sight.

That ring had to be the most valuable thing in her possession. But she wanted to make sure that her metal detector was working properly. And she was so intent on finding all the lost treasures out in the beach that she was willing to let that ring go. She was willing to risk it, to lose it in order to find it again. All for the sake of finding every other lost thing on the beach.

Sure enough, after a few sweeps, she found that precious ring again. And she was even more determined to continue her search.

Since the beginning of the human story, God has been on a search for every lost soul. Every person wandering in darkness, desperate to be found. And what happened on Good Friday is that God was willing to lose God's most prized possession—God's very own self in Jesus, to be buried deep within the sands of sin.

But on that first Easter, God raised Jesus from the burial of death. To prove that God's power to search and rescue was perfect. And ever since, God has been searching for you.

> *On that first Easter, God raised*
> *Jesus from the burial of death.*
> *To prove that God's power to search*
> *and rescue was perfect. And ever since,*
> *God has been searching for you.*

After that woman put the ring back on her finger and continued sweeping. And then she stopped. She heard a beep. And she bent down with her strainer basket and started to sift.

I couldn't tell what she found. I only saw that she stuck it in her pocket.

But we know what humanity found that first Sunday morning. It was new life, through the resurrection of Jesus. And just as Jesus called Mary by name in John's Easter story, God is whispering your name today.

This great God of the universe knows you and is calling you by name today. And God has gone to great lengths today to find you, claim you, and bring you back home. You may have felt like your life has been stolen away.

But God has brought you back and given you salvation.

Now it is up to you: What will you do with it?

CHRISTUS VICTOR IN SUMMARY

Definition of Sin: Sin weighs us down and renders us powerless to overcome it on our own strength. We are left in a perpetual state of being defeated, as if we were doomed to push a boulder uphill every day.

Definition of Salvation: Just like God rolled away the stone, Jesus grants us victory over sin and enables us to overcome the sins in our lives.

Pros: Christus Victor is celebrative, joyful, and life-affirming by its nature. It can be especially helpful for those who feel defeated by sin and provides a helpful alternative to violent imagery in the other atonement theories.

Cons: Like the ransom theory, it can be construed as rendering so much power to sin that it suggests a dualistic worldview, in which God and evil are dueling foes.

Response: We are called to live in the victory that Jesus provides, and rather than take our freedom for granted, use it to love God and others.

REFLECTING ON THE CROSS

Because you have been saved by God in Christ, what will you do with the freedom, restoration, and victory that God has given you? What difference will that make in your life and in the lives of others?

How will you participate in God's ongoing work of defeating violence with nonviolence?

Which of the atonement theories were new to you? Which ones piqued your interest? And which ones do you find most helpful in shaping the way you think and act?

NOTES

Chapter 1

"He Took My Place," https://hymnary.org/text/a_trembling_soul_i
_sought_the_lord. Accessed October 8, 2020.

1 Bill Watterson, *Calvin and Hobbes Tenth Anniversary Edition* (Kansas
City, MO: Andrews and McMeel, 1995).

2 Positive and negative commandments of the Torah, https://www
.chabad.org/library/article_cdo/aid/901695/jewish/Positive
-Commandments.htm, https://www.chabad.org/library/article
_cdo/aid/901723/jewish/Negative-Commandments.htm. Accessed
October 8, 2020.

3 "Captain Coutts' Last Chance," *Don Dorrigo Gazette*, June 28, 1924,
https://trove.nla.gov.au/newspaper/article/171875403. Accessed
September 15, 2020.

4 Edward Fairweather, ed. and trans., *A Scholastic Miscellany: Anselm
to Ockham*, vol. 10, The Library of Christian Classics (London: SCM
Press, 1956), 120. Also, *Christian Believer: Knowing God with Heart
and Mind: Readings* (Nashville: Abingdon Press 1999), 127.

5 *Christian Believer*, 130. Also, John Calvin, *Institutes of Christian
Religion*, chap. 12, section 3, https://www.biblestudytools.com
/history/calvin-institutes-christianity/book2/chapter-12.html.
Accessed September 15, 2020.

6 Anonymous, *The United Methodist Hymnal* (Nashville: The United
Methodist Publishing House, 1989), 286, stanzas 1 and 2.

7   "A Service of Word and Table I," *The United Methodist Hymnal*, (Nashville: The United Methodist Publishing House), 10.

8   Fanny J. Crosby, *The United Methodist Hymnal*, 98, stanza 2 and refrain.

9   C. S. Lewis, *The Lion, the Witch and the Wardrobe* (New York: Harper Collins, 2005), 141–42.

10 Lewis, *The Lion, the Witch and the Wardrobe*, 163.

11 Dallas Willard, *The Great Omission: Reclaiming Jesus's Essential Teachings on Discipleship* (New York: HarperCollins, 2016), 14.

Chapter 2

1   *Christian Believer*, 125.

2   "A Sermon of the Salvation of Mankind, by only Christ our Savior, from Sin and Death everlasting" *Sermons or Homilies Appointed to be Read in Churches in the time of Queen Elizabeth of Famous Memory: In Two Parts, to which are Added, the Constitutions and Canons Ecclesiastical and the Thirty-nine Articles of the Church of England*, (Oxford, United Kingdom: Clarendon Press, 1816), 19.

3   George Johnson, "Healing Religions Harm" (lecture, Luther Seminary, St. Paul, MN, July 2005).

4   From Daniel Rothenberg, *With These Hands: The Hidden World of Migrant Farm Workers Today* (Berkeley: University of California Press, 1998), xi–xii.

5   "Green Finch and Linnet Bird," by Stephen Sondheim, https://genius.com/Stephen-sondheim-green-finch-and-linnet-bird-lyrics. Accessed October 4, 2020.

6   Laura Story, "Blessings," track # 5 on *Blessings*, Fair Trade Services, 2011, CD.

7   Ben Weir, *Hostage Bound, Hostage Free* (Philadelphia: Westminster Press, 1987), 31.

Chapter 3

1   Peter Abelard, *Commentary on the Epistle to the Romans* (Washington, DC: The Catholic University of America Press, 2011), 161-63. Project MUSE, muse.jhu.edu/book/18677. Accessed September 15, 2020.

2   Óscar Arnulfo Romero, *Saint Oscar Romero: Voice of the Voiceless: The Four Pastoral Letters and Other Statements* (Maryknoll, NY: Orbis, 1985, 2020), loc. 4487, Kindle.

3   Óscar Arnulfo Romero, *The Violence of Love* (Maryknoll, NY: Orbis, 2004), 25.

Chapter 4

1   Frank Logue, *A Season of Healing: 365 Readings A Year-Long Journey Toward Wholeness*, Day 68, http://kingofpeace.org/aseasonofhealing .pdf. Accessed September 15, 2020.

2   *Augustine*, from Philip Schaff, ed. 1998 (Grand Rapids: Eerdmans, 1998), 272.

3   Steve Hartman, "Best friends with 'the same soul' swear they're twins," *CBS Evening News*, July 12, 2019. https://www.cbsnews .com/news/best-friends-with-the-same-soul-swear-they-are -twins-2019-07-12/. Accessed October 6, 2020.

Chapter 5

     The United Methodist Hymnal, 365, stanza 3.

1   Imre Zoltán, "Ignaz Semmelweis" in *Encyclopædia Britannica*, published August 9, 2020, https://www.britannica.com/biography /Ignaz-Semmelweis. Accessed September 17, 2020.

2   Tertullian, "A Treatise on the Soul," chap. 40, https://www.newadvent .org/fathers/0310.htm. Accessed October 6, 2020.

3   Gerald Bray and Thomas C. Oden, eds., *Ancient Christian Commentary on the Scriptures: Romans* (Downer's Grove, IL: IVP Academic, 2005), 101.

4   Bray and Oden, eds., *Ancient Christian Commentary on the Scriptures,* 102.

5   Flannery O'Connor, *A Prayer Journal* (New York: Farrar, Straus and Giroux, 2013), 3–4.

6   Morton T. Kelsey, "The Cross and the Cellar," in *Bread and Wine: Readings for Lent and Easter* (Walden, NY: Plough Publishing House, 2003), 210-11.

Chapter 6

1   *Christian Believer*, #144, 119.
2   Alister McGrath, *What Was God Doing on the Cross?* (Eugene, OR: Wipf and Stock, 2003).
3   Eugene M. Bartlett, "Victory in Jesus," *The United Methodist Hymnal*, 370.
4   Walter Wink, *The Powers that Be: Theology for a New Millennium* (New York: Galilee, 1999), 69.
5   S. Mark Heim, *Saved from Sacrifice: A Theology of the Cross*, (Grand Rapids: Eerdmans, 2006), 329.

CPSIA information can be obtained
at www.ICGtesting.com
Printed in the USA
LVHW020157040122
707695LV00006B/13